THE BATTLE FOR THE CHRISTIAN MIND

BE TRANSFORMED BY THE RENEWAL OF YOUR MIND

RENEW
your mind
Romans 12:2

EDWARD D. ANDREWS

"Be renewed in the spirit of
your minds"—Ephesians 4:23

THE BATTLE FOR THE CHRISTIAN MIND

Be Transformed by the Renewal of Your Mind

Edward D. Andrews

Christian Publishing House

Cambridge, Ohio

CHRISTIAN
PUBLISHING
HOUSE

FOUNDED 2005

THE BATTLE FOR THE CHRISTIAN MIND: *Be Transformed by the Renewal of Your Mind* by Edward D. Andrews

ISBN-10: 1945757264

ISBN-13: 978-1945757266

Table of Contents

Edward D. Andrews

Book Description

In the earnest and thought-provoking work, "THE BATTLE FOR THE CHRISTIAN MIND: Be Transformed by the Renewal of Your Mind," readers are invited to embark on a crucial journey towards spiritual clarity and resilience. The book dives into the complexities of the Christian mind, grappling with the profound effects of sin, the importance of a sound mindset, and the transformative power of Scripture.

Detailed, Insightful, and Rooted in Scripture. With each chapter, the author meticulously delves into the intrinsic battle faced by every believer—the struggle between a sinful nature and the quest for divine truth. From the origins of sin found in the Garden of Eden to the practical steps towards embodying the mind of Christ, this book acts as a guide for readers to navigate through the tumultuous spiritual terrain that defines our times.

A Scholarly Approach to Christian Living. The author, employing a rigorously scriptural lens, dissects the very fabric of human imperfection, examining its impact on our daily lives and our relationship with God. Through an exploration of biblical figures, readers gain insight into the redemptive potential for their own lives, learning how the wisdom of the past can inform the challenges of the present.

Mental Discipline and Spiritual Warfare. "The Battle for the Christian Mind" does not shy away from addressing the often-overlooked aspects of spiritual warfare. By equipping readers with the "Sword of the Spirit" and offering strategies for maintaining a Christian mindset in a secular world, the book empowers believers to safeguard their thoughts against the deceptions of the evil one.

The Controversial Topic of the Holy Spirit's Indwelling. A defining feature of the text is its nuanced discussion on the indwelling of the Holy Spirit. Without resorting to common misconceptions, the author lays a clear framework for understanding the Spirit's true

8

influence through Scripture—eschewing the idea of a mystical indwelling and promoting a grounded, biblical view of spiritual growth.

For the Skeptical and the Seeking. Whether one is skeptical of contemporary Christian thought or seeking a deeper, more authentic practice of faith, this book offers a wellspring of wisdom. It is an essential read for those who yearn to align their thoughts with the will of God, aiming to live a life marked by spiritual insight and unwavering devotion.

An Anchor in the Storm. In an age marked by confusion and spiritual malaise, "THE BATTLE FOR THE CHRISTIAN MIND: Be Transformed by the Renewal of Your Mind" stands as an anchor, calling believers back to the solid ground of Scripture. It is an invaluable resource for anyone eager to fortify their mind with the truths that have stood the test of time.

This book is not merely a collection of theological musings but a call to action—a meticulous blueprint for waging and winning the battle for the Christian mind.

Edward D. Andrews

Preface

Welcome to "THE BATTLE FOR THE CHRISTIAN MIND: Be Transformed by the Renewal of Your Mind." This book is more than an exploration; it's a call to arms, an invitation to engage in the most critical conflict we face as believers—the warfare for our thoughts and by extension, our very souls.

At the core of this book lies a fundamental question: How does one cultivate a mindset that reflects the teachings and spirit of Christ amidst a world that often seems diametrically opposed to it? In seeking to answer this, we will traverse through the complex interplay between our inherent sinful nature and the transformative power of God's Word.

Our journey begins with an unflinching examination of the sin-entrenched human condition. It's a condition that casts a long shadow over our actions and decisions, one that has repercussions that resonate through our relationship with God and with each other. Yet, through the Scriptures, we uncover a pathway to not just understanding but overcoming these inborn imperfections.

In the following chapters, we turn our attention to what it means to possess the "mind of Christ." This is not merely an academic pursuit. It requires humility, discipline, and a steadfast commitment to living in a manner that honors Christ. We will dissect what sound-mindedness entails and how to guard against the corrupting influences that besiege us daily.

The concept of transformation occupies a central role in our discourse. This metamorphosis is not a momentary change but a lifelong process, nourished through the continuous study of Scripture and heartfelt prayer. We will witness the transformation in the lives of biblical figures, drawing from their experiences, strength, and encouragement for our spiritual journey.

A pivotal topic this book addresses is the indwelling of the Holy Spirit—a subject of much debate and misunderstanding within

Christendom. By returning to a biblical understanding, we clarify misconceptions, guiding readers to a more scripturally anchored interpretation of the Spirit's work within us.

As the author, my objective has been to present these complex theological issues in a manner accessible to all—eschewing scholarly jargon in favor of clarity and practicality. I hope to equip you, the reader, with the knowledge and understanding necessary to not just engage in the battle for your mind but to emerge victorious.

The insights shared herein are the culmination of years of study, reflection, and a deep-seated commitment to the integrity of Scripture. It is my prayer that "THE BATTLE FOR THE CHRISTIAN MIND" serves as a beacon, illuminating your path as you endeavor to renew your mind and live out the transformative power of the Gospel.

May this book inspire you to take up your shield of faith, wield the sword of the Spirit, and stand firm in the knowledge of God's Word as we together strive to think and live in a way that is pleasing to our Lord and Savior, Jesus Christ.

Edward D. Andrews

Author of 220+ books and Chie Translator of the Updated American Standard Version

Introduction

In the tapestry of Christian life, the mind is the battlefield where our greatest spiritual contests are waged. Thoughts and beliefs shape actions, and actions become the milestones of our faith journey. The struggle is intense, relentless, and personal. It's here, in the recesses of our thoughts, where "THE BATTLE FOR THE CHRISTIAN MIND: Be Transformed by the Renewal of Your Mind" seeks to serve as a crucial ally.

This book is not an academic treatise disconnected from the day-to-day realities of faith. Instead, it is a manual for those who yearn to align their thinking with the timeless truths of Scripture. As we embark on this journey together, it's important to understand what this book is and what it hopes to accomplish.

The Christian mind is the fulcrum of one's spiritual health and vitality. It can be a wellspring of life when grounded in biblical truth or a source of turmoil when influenced by the deceit of the world and our own flawed nature. Herein lies our central thesis: The mind influenced by Scripture is the fortress that withstands the onslaught of moral relativism, secular ideologies, and the subtleties of spiritual deception that characterize our age.

In this introduction, we set the stage for a transformative experience. We confront the reality of our sinful nature and the profound need for redemption and renewal. It's a theme that runs throughout the fabric of the Scriptures—humans, created in the image of God, now marred by sin, seeking restoration through divine intervention.

As we delve into these pages, we do so with the understanding that knowledge alone is insufficient. The Pharisees had knowledge, yet their hearts were far from God. It's not just about filling our heads with information but allowing that knowledge to penetrate deep into our hearts, manifesting in a life that bears fruit in keeping with repentance.

Each chapter of this book is designed to build upon the previous, leading us into a deeper, more robust understanding of what it means to have the mind of Christ. We navigate through the complexities of the spiritual maladies that afflict us, diagnosing the symptoms and prescribing the biblical remedy. We confront self-defeating thoughts and learn to counter them with the power and clarity of God's Word.

This is a call to spiritual sobriety and vigilance. The pages that follow are meant to equip you with the spiritual discernment necessary to distinguish truth from error, to understand the profound realities of Scripture, and to embrace them not just intellectually but experientially.

I invite you, dear reader, to approach this book not as a passive observer but as an active participant in the battle for your mind. Engage with the Scriptures presented, reflect on the principles discussed, and apply the truths learned. As Romans 12:2 reminds us, the transformation we seek is not conformation to this world but a metamorphosis achieved by the renewal of our mind—a renewal that enables us to discern God's good, pleasing, and perfect will.

With prayerful expectation, let us step into the fray, equipped with the full armor of God, ready to be transformed by the renewal of our minds. Let the battle begin.

CHAPTER 1 We are All Born with a Sinful Nature

The Origin of Sin: Tracing Back to Adam and Eve

The narrative of sin's entry into the human experience is intricately woven into the fabric of biblical theology and history. As we delve into the roots of humanity's sinful nature, we trace the line back to the very beginning, to the Garden of Eden, where the first humans, Adam and Eve, resided. The Hebrew text of Genesis, specifically Genesis 2:17, introduces us to the command given by Jehovah to Adam regarding the tree of the knowledge of good and evil, "but from the tree of the knowledge of good and evil you shall not eat, for in the day that you eat from it you will surely die." This command sets the stage for the pivotal moment in human history.

Adam and Eve's decision to eat from this forbidden tree, as depicted in Genesis 3, is the act that inaugurates the sinful condition of the human race—a condition that has been inherited by all of Adam's progeny. The Hebrew word for sin, *chatta'ah*, implies missing the mark or straying from the correct path. The Greek equivalent used in the New Testament, *hamartia*, carries a similar connotation. When Adam and Eve chose to disobey, they missed the mark set by Jehovah's standards, thereby altering the spiritual state of humanity.

The *fall*, as this event is commonly referred to, is not merely an isolated incident of disobedience; it signifies a fundamental change in the relationship between humanity and God. Romans 5:12, written in Greek, explains this: "Therefore, just as through one man sin entered into the world, and death through sin, so death spread to all men because all sinned." Here the apostle Paul is highlighting the universal impact of Adam's sin. The term "world" (*kosmos* in Greek) reflects the comprehensive scope of sin's reach, encompassing all of creation and every human born into it.

Adam, formed from the dust of the ground as a living *nephesh* (soul) according to Genesis 2:7, was created with free will, able to choose obedience or disobedience. This same capacity is evident in Eve's interaction with the serpent. It is this very ability to choose that underlies the human predicament. When Adam and Eve exercised their free will to disobey Jehovah, they set a precedent for human nature—a predisposition towards rebellion and a propensity for sin.

The effects of their choice were immediate and far-reaching. Not only did they experience a spiritual death—separation from Jehovah—but they also initiated a process of physical decay, leading to eventual physical death. The imagery of decay and death permeates the biblical narrative as a constant reminder of the pervasive effects of sin.

The nature of sin is such that it acts like a contagion, an inherited trait passed on from generation to generation. This hereditary aspect of sin is often misunderstood; it is not that we are guilty of Adam's sin, but rather, as the Psalmist declares in Psalm 51:5, we are born with an inherent sinful disposition: "Behold, I was brought forth in error, and in sin my mother conceived me." The term *error* (*'avon* in Hebrew) suggests a bent or a tendency toward deviance, an inborn inclination that each individual must wrestle with.

Furthermore, the sin of Adam and Eve introduced a distortion in the human intellect and will—a *noetic effect* of sin—which impacts our ability to think, reason, and choose rightly. The apostle Paul in Romans 1:21-22 outlines the degradation of human reasoning as a result of sin, illustrating how even the wise can become foolish when they exchange the glory of the immortal God for images resembling mortal man.

The profound truth is that every human being is born into a world that is marked by the stain of the first sin. Our very nature is tarnished by it, and our thoughts, as well as our actions, are inclined towards evil. Yet, Jehovah provided a means of redemption, a path to restore the broken relationship between Himself and humanity. This redemptive narrative unfolds throughout the Scriptures, culminating in the person and work of Jesus Christ, who offers salvation and the possibility of a renewed mind.

The task of Christian counseling, therefore, is not merely to address the behavioral symptoms of sin but to recognize and confront the underlying sinful nature that plagues all individuals. It involves guiding counselees to understand their intrinsic need for the transformation that comes from a relationship with Christ. Romans 12:2 encapsulates this transformational process: "And do not be conformed to this world, but be transformed by the renewal of your mind, so that you may prove what the will of God is, that which is good and acceptable and perfect." The Greek word for "transformed" (*metamorphoō*) suggests a profound and complete change, akin to the metamorphosis of a caterpillar into a butterfly. It is a radical reorientation from a mind bent on sin to one that is aligned with the will and purposes of Jehovah.

As we ponder the depths of sin's origin and its effects, we recognize that the battle for the Christian mind is fundamentally a battle against this inherited sinful nature. It is a daily struggle to choose obedience to Jehovah's standards, to live in a way that reflects His righteousness rather than succumbing to the inherent sinfulness that vies for dominance. The call to be transformed by the renewal of our minds is a call to engage in this battle wholeheartedly, armed with the Spirit-inspired Word of God, which is able to discern the thoughts and intentions of the heart (Hebrews 4:12).

In summary, the origin of sin in the human experience can be traced back to the pivotal moment in the Garden of Eden. This hereditary nature of sin affects every aspect of our being, requiring a profound transformation—a renewal of the mind that aligns us with Jehovah's will and purposes, a process that is central to the Christian faith and the life of every believer.

Recognizing Our Inherited Imperfection

The struggle for the Christian mind begins with acknowledging a fundamental biblical truth: all humans inherit a nature deeply flawed and predisposed toward sin. This is not a superficial blemish that can be scrubbed clean with good intentions or moral deeds; it is a profound spiritual imperfection rooted in the earliest chapters of human history.

The Human Condition as Presented in Scripture

The biblical narrative paints a stark picture of humanity's spiritual trajectory. From the moment Adam and Eve disobeyed Jehovah's command in the Garden of Eden (Genesis 3), sin became an indelible part of the human fabric. This original act of disobedience, often referred to as *original sin*, had repercussions that extended beyond the individuals involved. It signified the corruption of human nature, a corruption that would be passed down through every generation.

The Old Testament frequently touches on the pervasiveness of this inherited imperfection. For instance, Genesis 6:5 reveals the extent of human wickedness when it states, "Then Jehovah saw that the wickedness of man was great on the earth, and that every intent of the thoughts of his heart was only evil continually." The Hebrew term for "intent" (*yetser*) and for "thoughts" (*machashabah*) here suggest a shaping or fashioning of the innermost attitudes and plans. This portrayal is not merely of occasional lapses into wrongdoing; it depicts a consistent, all-encompassing inclination towards evil.

Similarly, Genesis 8:21 acknowledges the enduring nature of man's sinful predisposition, even from youth. Jeremiah the prophet, in Jeremiah 17:9, presents a dire diagnosis of the human heart: "The heart is more deceitful than all else and is desperately sick; who can understand it?" The Hebrew phrase used for "deceitful" (*'aqov*) indicates something twisted or crooked, emphasizing the internal and unknowable depth of humanity's treachery against divine standards.

The New Testament's Continuation of the Theme

The New Testament writers continue to expound on this theme of an inherent sin nature. The apostle Paul, in his epistles, often addresses the inner conflict and the natural human inclination toward sin. In Romans 7:18, he candidly admits, "For I know that nothing good dwells in me, that is, in my flesh; for the willing is present in me, but the doing of the good is not." Here, Paul uses the term "flesh" (*sarx* in Greek) to symbolize the sinful human nature that opposes spiritual truths.

This struggle is not isolated to behavior alone but extends to the mind as well. In Romans 8:7, Paul explains, "because the mind set on the flesh is hostile toward God; for it does not subject itself to the law of God, for it is not even able to do so." The Greek term for "mind" (*phronema*) denotes not just intellectual activity, but also the inclinations and purposes of the individual. It underscores the depth of the spiritual malaise that afflicts the human condition, a malaise that affects our very reasoning and capacity for spiritual understanding.

Inherited Imperfection and the Conscience

The Bible acknowledges that all humans are born with a conscience, an inherent sense of right and wrong. However, due to our inherited imperfection, this moral compass is not sufficient to guide us to perfect thoughts and actions. Paul elaborates on the role of the conscience among Gentiles who do not have the Law in Romans 2:14-15, explaining that their consciences alternatively accuse or defend their actions. Yet, without the transforming power of God's Word, the conscience can become seared, as implied in 1 Timothy 4:2, where Paul speaks of those whose consciences are "branded as with a hot iron." The conscience, then, while a gift from God, is not immune to the corrupting influence of our sinful nature.

Mental Renewal Through the Word of God

It is within this context that Paul's exhortation in Romans 12:2 must be understood. The renewal of the mind is not a passive process but an active transformation necessitated by our inherited imperfection. This renewal is not accomplished through human effort alone but through engagement with the "Spirit-inspired Word of God," which is sharper than any two-edged sword, piercing between soul and spirit (Hebrews 4:12). It is through the Word that Christians are equipped to fight against the mental strongholds established by sin.

The mental battle that Paul refers to in 2 Corinthians 10:4-5 is not fought with the weapons of the world but with divine power capable of demolishing strongholds. The "strongholds" here represent deeply ingrained patterns of thinking that stand opposed to the knowledge of God. Paul uses military imagery to depict the intensity of the conflict and the power of the weapons at the disposal of the believer, which are potent in God for pulling down these entrenched fortresses.

The Implications for Christian Counseling

In biblical Christian counseling, recognizing our inherited imperfection is crucial. It frames the understanding of every issue counselees may face, from interpersonal conflicts to deep-seated personal struggles. Counselors must approach each situation with the awareness that the root of many problems lies within this flawed human nature. By redirecting counselees to the transformative power of Scripture and the necessity of mental renewal, counselors aim to help individuals align their thoughts and behaviors with Jehovah's will.

In conclusion, recognizing our inherited imperfection is the first step in the battle for the Christian mind. This recognition is not meant to lead to despair but to a realistic understanding of the human condition as presented in the Bible. With this understanding, Christians are called to seek the renewal of their minds, engaging with God's Word to overcome the flawed patterns of thinking inherent in our fallen nature, and to strive toward the mind of Christ, embodying the virtues and righteousness that come from God.

The Effects of Sin on Our Decisions and Actions

In the tapestry of human existence, each thread represents a decision or action. The vibrancy of its colors and the integrity of its weave are contingent upon the nature of those decisions and actions, which are invariably colored by sin's pervasive influence. This fundamental flaw, a sinful nature, is not merely a stain upon the individual threads; it is woven into the very fibers of the human soul.

The Biblical Paradigm of Sin's Impact

From the earliest pages of Scripture, the effects of sin on human decision-making and behavior are evident. When Adam and Eve chose to eat the forbidden fruit (Genesis 3), they initiated a legacy of corrupted autonomy, demonstrating how sin could twist the power of choice, which Jehovah had bestowed upon humanity. This pivotal moment underscores a profound truth: sin alters our decision-making at its core, influencing actions in ways that are contrary to God's will.

The Old Testament word for sin, *chatta'ah* (חַטָּאָה), implies more than just wrongdoing; it conveys the idea of missing the mark, as an archer might miss a target. This image is a powerful metaphor for understanding the nature of sin: it is a deviation from the standard of perfection established by Jehovah, a standard that humans, in their flawed condition, continually fail to meet.

In the New Testament, the Greek word for sin, *hamartia* (ἁμαρτία), carries a similar meaning. It, too, speaks of falling short or missing the mark, especially in relation to God and His laws. Every decision tainted by sin is thus a misstep, a divergence from the path of righteousness.

Sin's Effect on the Will and Conscience

Sin affects the will, our inner capacity to choose. The apostle Paul speaks to this in Romans 7:15-19, where he describes the agonizing struggle between the desire to do good and the overpowering inclination toward evil. He personifies sin as an almost separate entity that wages war against the law of the mind, leading to captivity to the law of sin (Romans 7:23).

The conscience, that inner sense of right and wrong given by God, is likewise compromised. Though it was designed to serve as a moral compass, the sinful nature dulls its precision. In Titus 1:15, Paul observes, "To the pure, all things are pure; but to those who are defiled and unbelieving, nothing is pure, but both their mind and their conscience are defiled." Here, the Greek term for "defiled" (*mianthosin* - μιαίνω) suggests a staining or polluting, depicting the conscience as no longer a reliable guide due to sin's contamination.

The Deceptive Nature of Sin

The Hebrew Bible offers profound insights into the deceptive nature of sin. Jeremiah the prophet describes the heart as "deceitful above all things" (*'aqov* - עָקֹב), which can mean crooked or distorted (Jeremiah 17:9). This deceitfulness signifies that the heart—representing the seat of human emotion and volition—is so corrupt that it can mislead the very person to whom it belongs. It can rationalize evil, repaint sin with the varnish of virtue, and justify the unjustifiable. Hence, decisions and actions become self-deceptive, leading one away from truth.

The Consequence of Sin on Actions

The tangible consequences of sin on human actions are vividly depicted throughout the Bible. For example, King David's decision to commit adultery with Bathsheba and his subsequent attempt to cover his sin led to a series of devastating outcomes, including murder and familial strife (2 Samuel 11-12). David's choices, under the influence of sin, brought about dire repercussions that rippled through his life and reign.

In the New Testament, the Gospels record the Pharisees' hardened hearts, which led to their constant opposition to Jesus' ministry. Their inability to recognize the Messiah was a direct result of sin blinding their spiritual perception. They epitomize the New Testament warning of how sin can harden the heart, as noted in Hebrews 3:13, where believers are cautioned against being hardened by the deceitfulness of sin.

Sin's Subversion of Human Rationality

Sin does not only prompt humans to make poor decisions; it also skews the rational process by which those decisions are made. This is reflected in Paul's message to the Corinthians about the natural person not accepting the things of the Spirit of God, for they are *moria* (μωρία) to him, which means foolishness (1 Corinthians 2:14). Here, the term *moria* illuminates how sin can make divine wisdom appear as folly to

21

the human mind, thereby subverting the very criteria by which we judge truth and error.

Overcoming Sin's Influence

While sin's effects are profound and pervasive, the biblical narrative does not leave humanity in a hopeless cycle of sin and failure. Instead, it presents the possibility of transformation through the renewal of the mind, as detailed in Romans 12:2. The Greek word for transformation here, *metamorphoo* (μεταμορφόω), describes a complete change, akin to a caterpillar becoming a butterfly. This metamorphosis is possible not through human effort alone but through the power of the Spirit-inspired Word of God. The renewal of the mind is a process by which the believer, guided by Scripture, learns to discern Jehovah's will, which is good, acceptable, and perfect.

In conclusion, sin's impact on our decisions and actions is profound and multifaceted. It corrupts the human will, defiles the conscience, deceives the heart, brings destructive consequences, and subverts rationality. However, through the Scripture's wisdom and the application of its truths, believers can engage in the battle for the Christian mind, fighting against sin's influence and moving toward the life that reflects the holiness and righteousness of God.

Overcoming Our Sinful Tendencies Through Scriptural Guidance

In grappling with the formidable presence of sin in the human condition, we acknowledge that our proclivities towards sinful behavior are not merely circumstantial, but stem from a fundamental inclination within our nature. From the very onset of life, individuals carry the weight of an inherent sinful disposition, a *yetzer ra* (יצר רע), a concept captured in the Hebrew texts of Genesis 6:5 and 8:21, denoting an innate tendency towards evil. It is within this context that we must examine the transformative power of Scripture to guide and reform the believer's mind, aligning it more closely with the mind of Christ.

The Sinful Mind vs. The Mind of Christ

The apostle Paul brings to light the dichotomy between the sinful mind and the mind of Christ in his epistles. In Romans 8:5-7, Paul contrasts those who live according to the sinful nature with those who live in accordance with the Spirit. The Greek term *phronema* (φρόνημα) of the flesh signifies a mindset or perspective, indicative of a deeper spiritual reality that governs behavior. This inherent *phronema* of the flesh is antithetical to God's law; it cannot submit to Jehovah's righteous decrees.

Yet, there is a profound transformation that occurs when one is guided by Scripture. In Philippians 2:5, the exhortation is clear: "Let this mind be in you, which was also in Christ Jesus." The term *phroneite* (φρονεῖτε) calls for the adoption of an outlook or attitude that mirrors that of Jesus—a lowliness of mind and a unity of purpose with fellow believers.

Strengthening the Conscience Through Scripture

Every person is endowed with a conscience, a moral compass that Jehovah God has embedded within us. However, this conscience, without the guiding light of Scripture, can become seared or hardened, as expressed by the term *kausteriazo* (καυστηριάζω) used in 1 Timothy 4:2. A Christian must, therefore, nurture and fortify the conscience with the divine wisdom of the Bible to ensure it remains sensitive and operative.

The Peril of Ignored Conscience

Ignoring the conscience can lead to a perilous state where the heart becomes increasingly callous. This is highlighted in Ephesians 4:17-19, where Paul describes Gentiles who are estranged from the life of God due to the ignorance and hardness of their hearts. He uses the term *porosis* (πώρωσις) to depict this hardening, a term that carries the connotation of petrification, illustrating how the human heart can become stone-like, impervious to spiritual truths.

Cultivating Biblical Mindedness

To cultivate a biblical mindset is to engage actively in the process outlined in Romans 12:2, which speaks of being transformed by the renewing of the mind. The term *metamorphoo* (μεταμορφόω), as previously mentioned, is a call to a radical overhaul of one's thought patterns, aligning them with the righteousness and holiness of God. It is not a passive state but an active pursuit of godliness through the assimilation of scriptural principles.

Destroying Strongholds through Divine Power

Paul presents a vivid metaphor for the battle of the mind in 2 Corinthians 10:4, where he discusses the divine power that can demolish strongholds. These strongholds, *ochuromata* (ὀχυρώματα) in Greek, represent the deeply entrenched sin patterns and false reasoning that fortify themselves against the knowledge of God. It is through the application of God's Word that these fortifications are dismantled, enabling the believer to capture every thought and make it obedient to Christ (2 Corinthians 10:5).

Understanding vs. Embracing Divine Revelation

It is critical to discern between understanding Scripture and embracing its truths. The words translated as "understand" in 1 Corinthians 2:12 and "does not accept" in 1 Corinthians 2:14 are *ginosko* (γινώσκω) and *dechomai* (δέχομαι), respectively. The former suggests a cognitive comprehension, while the latter implies a welcoming or acceptance. Paul's argument is not that the unbeliever is incapable of comprehending Scripture, but rather that they do not welcome or embrace its truths, seeing them as *moria* (μωρία)—folly, and thus reject them.

The Role of the Spirit-Inspired Word

While some traditions hold that the Holy Spirit indwells believers to guide them into all truth, the perspective outlined in this chapter emphasizes that it is through the Spirit-inspired Word of God that guidance is received. The Spirit does not indwell in the manner of mystical experience but rather through the profound impact of Scripture on the believer's mind and heart.

In summary, overcoming our sinful tendencies is a process that involves a rigorous engagement with Scripture. It demands the strengthening of our conscience through the wisdom of the Word, the adoption of a mindset that mirrors Christ's humility and unity, and the active demolition of mental strongholds that oppose the knowledge of Jehovah. The embracing of divine revelation and the guidance of the Spirit-inspired Word are paramount in this struggle, highlighting the indispensable role of Scripture in the battle for the Christian mind.

Edward D. Andrews

CHAPTER 2 Fully Understanding Our Human Imperfection

Acknowledging Our Flawed Human Condition

In the earnest pursuit to grasp the full breadth of our human imperfection, it is crucial to begin by acknowledging that from the earliest pages of Scripture, humanity is depicted as inherently flawed and perpetually skewed towards a trajectory of rebellion against Jehovah God. The foundational texts of Genesis 6:5 and 8:21 render a sobering portrait of the human heart, marked by a propensity towards evil that permeates thought and action.

The Hebrew term used in Genesis, *yetzer* (יֵצֶר), denotes a formative force or inclination, and its coupling with *ra* (רַע), meaning "bad" or "evil," illustrates the internal and constant pull towards wrongdoing. This conception of an inborn inclination towards sin is not merely an abstract theological notion but a reality that manifests in various dimensions of human behavior and decision-making.

Within this frame, the prophet Jeremiah speaks poignantly of the human heart in Jeremiah 17:9, using the term *akob* (עָקֹב), which can be translated as "deceitful" or "crooked," and *anash* (אָנַשׁ), which carries the sense of "desperately sick." The heart, therefore, is not just fallible but is fundamentally enigmatic and treacherous, capable of leading one into paths that are destructive.

The apostle Paul, well-acquainted with the human struggle against sin, warned of the mind's vulnerability to the deceptive schemes of Satan. In his epistles, Paul often contrasts the mind governed by the flesh with the mind led by the Spirit. He uses terms such as *sarkikos* (σαρκικός) for "fleshly" and *pneumatikos* (πνευματικός) for "spiritual" to

26

draw this distinction. The former is susceptible to the corruption that is in the world because of sinful desire (2 Peter 1:4), while the latter aspires to the purity and obedience of Christ.

However, this condition is not left without remedy, for Paul presents the solution in Romans 12:2, advocating for a transformation, a *metanoia* (μετάνοια), through the renewal, *anakainosis* (ἀνακαίνωσις), of the mind. This renewal is not a mere adjustment but a complete overhaul of the internal structures of thought, emotion, and will, brought about by an immersion in the Word of God.

Furthermore, Paul elucidates the concept of conscience, which in Greek is referred to as *suneidēsis* (συνείδησις), a knowing-with oneself. The conscience acts as a moral barometer, yet without the calibration provided by scriptural truth, it can lead one astray. When fortified with the Scriptures, the conscience serves as a reliable guide toward the mind of Christ, *nous Christou* (νοῦς Χριστοῦ), which is characterized by humility and unity with fellow believers.

As believers strive for this Christ-like mindset, they encounter opposition not only from within but also from without, in the form of ideological strongholds that resist the knowledge of God. Paul speaks of the weapons of our warfare in 2 Corinthians 10:4, using the term *hopla* (ὅπλα) for "weapons" and *dunatos* (δυνατός), meaning "powerful," to describe the divine empowerment necessary to tear down these bastions of falsehood.

In the New Testament, the apostle Paul is conscious of the battleground that is the human mind, where the forces of truth and deception vie for dominance. His use of *logismos* (λογισμός), meaning "arguments" or "reasonings," in 2 Corinthians 10:5, underscores the intellectual aspect of this warfare, where every thought must be brought into captivity to the obedience of Christ.

The term *noema* (νόημα), often translated as "thought" or "mind," denotes not only the content of one's thoughts but also the intentions and purposes behind them. This is significant because it implies that our battle is not merely against errant thoughts but against the very intentions that give rise to them.

To fully embrace the Word of God, according to 1 Corinthians 2:14, requires more than intellectual assent; it necessitates a welcoming, a reception of spiritual truths into one's core being. The words "does not accept," "folly," and "not able to understand" illustrate the ways an unbeliever might reject divine revelation. Here, *dechomai* (δέχομαι) is translated as "does not accept," indicating a refusal to embrace; *mōria* (μωρία) denotes "folly" or "foolishness," signaling the dismissal of divine wisdom as irrational; and *gignōskō* (γινώσκω) in the form of "not able to understand" implies a failure to recognize or know intimately.

In this vein, the mind of the believer is called to a higher standard—a standard that acknowledges our flawed condition and turns to the Scriptures for renewal and guidance. The Spirit-inspired Word of God, rather than an indwelling Holy Spirit, becomes the compass by which believers navigate their imperfections and the moral and spiritual complexities of life.

In conclusion, recognizing our flawed human condition is not an end in itself but the starting point for a transformative journey. This journey is sustained by a steadfast engagement with the inspired Word, leading us to a profound transformation of the mind, aligning our thoughts, intents, and purposes with the divine will as revealed in the Holy Scriptures.

The Consequences of Imperfection on Our Relationship with God

The biblical narrative is replete with poignant reminders of the pervasive nature of human imperfection and its profound impact on our relationship with God. Genesis 6:5 reveals the depths of human depravity in its early stages, stating that "every intent of the thoughts of his heart was only evil continually." The word *yetzer* (יֵצֶר), referring to the "intent" or "inclination" of the human heart, is intrinsically bound to evil from youth, as stated in Genesis 8:21. This propensity disrupts the harmonious relationship humanity is meant to have with Jehovah God, as it stands in stark contrast to His holiness and purity.

Jeremiah 17:9 further elucidates the human condition by describing the heart as *akob* (עָקֹב), "deceitful," and *anash* (אָנֻשׁ),

28

"desperately sick." The duplicity and moral sickness of the human heart signify a barrier in understanding and aligning with God's will. The *lev*, the heart in Hebrew, is not just the seat of emotions but also the center of thought and decision-making, which is inherently flawed and unreliable in its natural state.

In the New Testament, the apostle Paul grapples with the dichotomy of the flesh and the spirit. He introduces a term *sarkikos* (σαρκικός), which symbolizes the human nature in its fallen state, to highlight the intrinsic conflict between our natural desires and God's righteous demands. This *sarkikos* mindset is at enmity with God, as it does not submit to God's law, nor can it do so (Romans 8:7).

The reality of this imperfection is not just a matter of moral failure but one that impacts the essence of communion with God. The sin that so easily entangles is a blockade that hinders our prayers, our worship, and our ability to fully grasp the profundities of divine truth. Isaiah's interaction with God in Isaiah 6:5 encapsulates this when he expresses a profound sense of unworthiness in the presence of Jehovah's holiness due to his *tamah* (טָמֵא), "unclean" lips, and the people's lips around him.

The consequences of this imperfection are multi-faceted. It engenders a spiritual separation from God, as sin creates a chasm between the Creator and the created. The notion of sin leading to death is not merely physical but spiritual as well, as seen in Romans 6:23. The *thanatos* (θάνατος), "death" Paul speaks of, symbolizes the ultimate consequence of sin—eternal separation from God.

Our conscience, a gift from God to guide us in moral discernment, also suffers under the weight of human imperfection. Paul mentions the conscience in 1 Corinthians 8:7, where the weaker conscience is susceptible to being defiled. The conscience, *suneidēsis* (συνείδησις) in Greek, can become seared, as mentioned in 1 Timothy 4:2, when continually ignored, losing its sensitivity to moral and spiritual truths.

Human imperfection also leads to distorted worldviews and ideologies that oppose the knowledge of God. In 2 Corinthians 10:4-5, Paul discusses the necessity of destroying these *ochuromata* (ὀχυρώματα), "strongholds," with divine weapons that have *dunamis* (δύναμις), "power" to demolish arguments and pretensions. These strongholds represent human reasoning that stands against the knowledge of God, and they must be taken captive to make every thought obedient to Christ.

A misaligned conscience and flawed reasoning further exacerbate the challenges believers face in understanding divine revelation. In 1 Corinthians 2:14, Paul uses the phrase *ou dechetai* (οὐ δέχεται), meaning "does not accept," to describe the natural person's rejection of the things of the Spirit of God. The wisdom of God is foolishness, *mōria* (μωρία), to him, and he is *ou dunatai gnonai* (οὐ δύναται γνῶναι), "not able to understand" them because they are spiritually discerned. This lack of understanding is not a mere intellectual deficit but a spiritual resistance to embracing the truths of God.

In the broader scheme of things, human imperfection impacts the collective testimony and unity of the body of Christ. The New Testament calls for a mindset that reflects Christ's humility and lowliness, a call often hampered by the pride and self-centeredness inherent in our flawed human nature. Philippians 2:5-8 exhorts believers to have the mind of Christ, who exemplified the ultimate standard of humility and obedience to God, a stark contrast to the natural inclination of the human mind.

However, the Scriptures also provide the remedy for this dire condition—transformation through the renewal of the mind. In Romans 12:2, Paul encourages believers not to conform to the pattern of this world but to be transformed by the *anakainosis* (ἀνακαίνωσις) of the mind, a complete renovation that realigns our thinking with God's will. This transformation is an ongoing process that requires continual exposure to and meditation on the Word of God.

To sum up, human imperfection deeply affects our relationship with God, obstructing our fellowship, distorting our conscience, and cultivating ideologies that are hostile to divine revelation. It also impairs our unity as believers and our individual spiritual growth. Nonetheless, God has provided His Word as the tool for the renewal of our minds, empowering us to break free from the chains of our inherent imperfections and to live a life that is pleasing to Him.

The Role of Repentance and Forgiveness

In the human experience, marked by imperfection and a proclivity toward wrongdoing, repentance and forgiveness stand as essential pillars for the restoration and transformation of the Christian mind. Repentance, from the Greek *metanoia* (μετάνοια), signifies a radical change of mind—a turning away from sin and a return to God. Forgiveness, or *aphesis* (ἄφεσις) in Greek, refers to the release from bondage or imprisonment, and in a biblical context, it implies the divine pardon of one's sins.

The Old Testament frequently addresses the theme of repentance, with the prophets calling the people of Israel to return to Jehovah. The prophet Hosea, for example, uses the imagery of returning to Jehovah and away from iniquity (Hosea 14:1-2). The act of turning back, or *shuv* (שׁוּב) in Hebrew, captures the essential movement of repentance—a conscious decision to change direction and seek reconciliation with God.

In the New Testament, Jesus Christ begins His public ministry with a call to repentance: "Repent, for the kingdom of heaven is at hand" (Matthew 4:17). The imperative *metanoeite* (μετανοεῖτε) underscores the urgency and necessity of a transformed mind and heart for those awaiting the Messiah's kingdom. It is not merely a call to feel sorrow for wrongdoing, but to exhibit a change that affects one's entire being and actions.

The parable of the Prodigal Son (Luke 15:11-32) serves as a vivid illustration of repentance and forgiveness. The son's return to his father after squandering his inheritance in reckless living is emblematic of *metanoia*. His acknowledgment of sin against heaven and before his father (Luke 15:21) exemplifies the acknowledgment necessary in repentance. The father's compassionate reception of the son, meanwhile, beautifully illustrates *aphesis*—not only is the son forgiven, but he is also restored to his place in the family.

Forgiveness is not simply a passive release from sin's penalty; it's an active restoration to righteousness. When Peter asks Jesus about the extent of forgiveness, Jesus replies with the parable of the unforgiving servant (Matthew 18:21-35), teaching that divine forgiveness of our debts is to be reflected in our forgiveness of others. This parable underscores the link between understanding one's own forgiveness and the imperative to forgive others. The servant who is forgiven a great debt yet fails to forgive a small debt owed to him by another is condemned for his lack of compassion, mirroring the expectation that those forgiven by God should extend forgiveness in turn.

Paul's epistles further elucidate the transformative nature of repentance and the power of forgiveness. In 2 Corinthians 7:10, Paul distinguishes between godly sorrow that produces *metanoia*, leading to salvation, and worldly sorrow, which brings death. Here, *lype* (λύπη), the sorrow that is according to the will of God, results in a radical change, not merely a feeling of remorse but a reorientation of life that aligns with God's will.

The practical outworking of repentance and forgiveness in the life of a Christian is the regeneration and renewal of the mind. Ephesians 4:22-24 calls believers to put off the old self, which is corrupt through deceitful desires, and to be renewed in the spirit of their minds. The *ananeousthai* (ἀνανεοῦσθαι) of the spirit of the mind involves a qualitative transformation, a renewal that is only possible through the *pneuma* (πνεῦμα), the Spirit-inspired Word of God.

In the realm of Christian counseling, repentance and forgiveness are not only theological concepts but also therapeutic tools. The guilt and shame associated with sin can create strongholds in the mind, leading to emotional and psychological distress. By embracing *metanoia*, individuals can find relief from the oppressive weight of these burdens. Similarly, extending *aphesis* to those who have wronged us can liberate us from cycles of anger and bitterness.

Forgiveness also has a communal aspect in the Christian experience. The early church's unity was predicated on the mutual forgiveness and acceptance that mirrored the grace they had received from Christ. Paul exhorts the Ephesian church to be kind to one another, tenderhearted, forgiving one another, as God in Christ forgave them (Ephesians 4:32). This *charizomenoi* (χαριζόμενοι), or gracious forgiveness, is not just an individual act but the fabric of a community that reflects the character of Christ.

A mind aligned with Christ is a mind that understands the depth of one's own sin, the breadth of God's forgiveness, and the height of the call to forgive others. Repentance and forgiveness are not one-time events but ongoing processes that continually reshape the believer's mind and heart. As Christians engage in this dual practice, they are drawn closer to the image of Christ and further from the corruption of their human imperfection. This transformative journey, while challenging, is the path to true freedom and peace for the Christian mind engaged in the battle against its inherent bent toward evil.

Striving for Perfection in an Imperfect World

In the pursuit of holiness within a world scarred by human imperfection, we are called to engage in a paradoxical endeavor. This pursuit is not one that suggests attainable perfection in our current state but rather a continuous striving toward the divine standard set forth by God. It is an aspirational journey, one that embodies the *teleios* (τέλειος) or completeness, maturity in Christ that the Scripture speaks of, particularly in the New Testament.

The Apostle Paul, well aware of the human condition, exhorts believers to strive toward being *teleios*, a term implying maturity and wholeness, which can sometimes be understood as perfection (Philippians 3:12-14). This striving is not about achieving sinlessness in this lifetime but about moving ever closer to the character and image of Christ. It is a pursuit that recognizes the gap between our present reality and the holiness of God, and it is driven by a desire to bridge that gap through spiritual growth and moral excellence.

This pursuit is further elucidated through the metaphor of the race set before us (Hebrews 12:1). The Christian life is compared to a long-distance race that requires endurance and discipline. Just as an athlete trains rigorously to compete, Christians are to exercise spiritual disciplines to grow in godliness. The Greek word *agonizomai* (ἀγωνίζομαι), often translated as "strive," carries with it the sense of struggling or contending for a prize. It's an active, intense effort that involves every aspect of one's being.

In this striving, the Sermon on the Mount stands as a pinnacle of ethical instruction. Jesus' statement, "You therefore must be perfect, as your heavenly Father is perfect" (Matthew 5:48), can seem like an insurmountable directive. Yet, when understood through the lens of biblical language, the term "perfect" (*teleios*) here implies a call to completeness in love, reflecting God's impartial love for all. This is not a call to flawless moral perfection but to a love that transcends natural human limitations and biases.

The believer's journey toward perfection is marked by the continuous practice of confession and repentance. The First Epistle of John assures believers that if we confess our sins, God is faithful and just to forgive us and to cleanse us from all unrighteousness (1 John 1:9). Confession, in Greek *homologia* (ὁμολογία), is an agreement with God about our sinfulness. It is a verbal acknowledgment that aligns our perspective with God's viewpoint of our imperfections. Repentance is not merely feeling remorse but entails a decisive change in direction, a turning away from sin and toward God.

The renewing of the mind, as mentioned in Romans 12:2, is crucial in this endeavor. The Greek for "renewing" (*anakainosis* - ἀνακαίνωσις) suggests a renovation or complete change for the better. The mind (*nous* - νοῦς) is the center of reasoning and moral understanding, and its renewal is necessary for discerning God's will, which is described as good, pleasing, and perfect. This process involves immersion in the Scriptures, prayer, and the application of God's Word to one's life.

Moreover, *koinonia* (κοινωνία), or fellowship with other believers, plays a significant role in our spiritual development. As iron sharpens iron, so one person sharpens another (Proverbs 27:17). The mutual encouragement and accountability found in the body of Christ are instrumental in our growth toward maturity.

However, this pursuit is often fraught with spiritual warfare. The Christian mind is the battlefield where truth contends with lies, holiness with sin, and faith with doubt. Paul's imagery of the armor of

God in Ephesians 6:10-18 is instructive here, portraying the need for divine strength and protection in the struggle against spiritual forces.

It is within this context that the concept of "destroying strongholds" in 2 Corinthians 10:4 finds its full expression. The *ochuromata* (ὀχυρώματα) or strongholds are the deeply entrenched patterns of thought that stand against the knowledge of God. Striving for perfection involves identifying these strongholds—whether they be pride, unforgiveness, lust, greed, or any other form of sin—and dismantling them through the power of God's Word.

The objective is not to achieve a sinless state but to be actively engaged in resisting sin and growing in grace. The Apostle Peter instructs believers to grow in the grace and knowledge of our Lord and Savior Jesus Christ (2 Peter 3:18). Growth implies a process; it is ongoing and directed toward an ultimate goal, which is the full knowledge (*epignosis* - ἐπίγνωσις) of Christ.

In conclusion, striving for perfection in an imperfect world is an arduous but noble pursuit, deeply rooted in the understanding of our human imperfection and the transforming power of God's Word. It is a journey that acknowledges our weaknesses but does not succumb to them, recognizing that while we may never reach sinless perfection in this life, we can continually move toward becoming more like Christ. This ongoing transformation shapes not only our actions but also our very minds, molding us into vessels fit for the Master's use, prepared for every good work (2 Timothy 2:21). Thus, the battle for the Christian mind is fought and won through steadfast perseverance, daily renewal, and an unwavering focus on the divine exemplar, our Lord Jesus Christ.

CHAPTER 3 Christians Must Be Sound in Mind

Defining Soundness of Mind from a Scriptural Perspective

The concept of "soundness of mind" in Scripture is multifaceted, encompassing rationality, self-control, wisdom, and spiritual discernment. It is a state of mental health and clarity aligned with divine wisdom and moral integrity.

Soundness of Mind as Rationality and Self-Control

The Greek term *sōphronismos* (σωφρονισμός), connoting soundness of mind, denotes a sound mental state that leads to self-control, moderation, and prudent behavior. This is apparent in the Pauline instruction for older men to be *sōphrōn* (Titus 2:2), reflecting a call for rationality and temperance. Rationality, in this sense, does not imply a cold, unfeeling logic but a reasoned approach to life that is moderated by faith. The self-control inherent in *sōphronismos* is the practical outworking of a sound mind—a mind that is aligned with God's will and reflects His character.

Wisdom as a Component of Soundness of Mind

In the biblical context, wisdom (*chokmah* in Hebrew, *sophia* in Greek) is more than intelligence or knowledge; it is the skillful living that comes from fearing Jehovah and obeying His commandments (Proverbs 9:10). A sound mind is thus inherently a wise mind, one that applies the knowledge of God's Word to daily life. Wisdom is the divine insight into the nature of things, granted by God, that informs right conduct.

Spiritual Discernment as Evidence of Soundness

Spiritual discernment (*diakrisis* in Greek) is the capability to distinguish between truth and error, right and wrong, holy and unholy. It is rooted in an intimate understanding of God's Word and is developed through constant practice. The Epistle to the Hebrews talks about those mature in faith as having their "senses exercised to discern both good and evil" (Hebrews 5:14). This discernment is crucial for a sound mind in a world where deceptive philosophies and ideologies abound.

The Mind of Christ as the Ideal

For Christians, the epitome of a sound mind is the mind of Christ (*nous Christou*). Paul's exhortation in 1 Corinthians 2:16 to have the mind of Christ is a call to a profound spiritual transformation that influences thoughts, attitudes, and actions. The mind of Christ is one that humbly submits to God's will and seeks to serve others, as seen in the life and ministry of Jesus. It is a mind that is not swayed by the temporal values of the world but is steadfastly fixed on eternal truths.

The Role of the Holy Spirit in Shaping the Mind

While there is no indwelling of the Holy Spirit, the Spirit-inspired Word of God plays a crucial role in shaping the mind. The Word of God is living and active, able to discern the thoughts and intentions of the heart (Hebrews 4:12). By engaging deeply with Scripture, Christians allow the truths contained within to mold their thinking and decision-making processes. The renewing of the mind that Paul speaks of in Romans 12:2 is a transformation that occurs as believers immerse themselves in the divine revelation of God's Word.

The Conscience and Soundness of Mind

The conscience, which Paul describes as bearing witness to our thoughts and actions (Romans 2:15), is a component of the mind that can either accuse or excuse us. A sound mind maintains a sensitive conscience, one that is strengthened and informed by the Word of

God. When the conscience is heeded, it serves as a guide that aligns our thoughts with God's moral standards. However, if ignored, it can become seared (1 Timothy 4:2), leading to moral insensitivity and spiritual decline.

Unification with Fellow Believers in Mind

The New Testament speaks to the importance of being of one mind with fellow believers (*auto phronēte* in Greek, Romans 12:16). This unity of mind is not about uniformity in thought but a shared commitment to Christ and the foundational truths of the faith. Such a unification in thought contributes to the soundness of the individual mind as it reflects the collective wisdom and support of the body of Christ.

Overcoming Mental Strongholds through Spiritual Warfare

In 2 Corinthians 10:4, the spiritual warfare against mental strongholds is about demolishing arguments and pretensions that set themselves up against the knowledge of God. This entails casting down imaginations (*logismous*) and every high thing that exalts itself against the knowledge of God (2 Corinthians 10:5). A sound mind is one that actively resists and overthrows such strongholds, replacing them with godly thoughts and attitudes.

The Role of Lowliness of Mind

In Philippians 2:3, Paul urges believers to do nothing out of selfish ambition or vain conceit but in lowliness of mind (*tapeinophrosynē*) esteem others better than themselves. This lowliness of mind is a humble recognition of one's limitations and a willingness to put the interests of others above one's own. It is a mental posture that rejects pride and embraces servanthood, mirroring the attitude of Christ.

Soundness of mind from a scriptural perspective is a rich and complex concept that incorporates rationality, self-control, wisdom, and spiritual discernment. It is rooted in a deep engagement with the

Word of God, a sensitive and informed conscience, and a humility that prioritizes unity and service over self-interest. The Christian pursuit of a sound mind is both a personal and communal endeavor, as believers seek to emulate the mind of Christ and engage in spiritual warfare to maintain mental integrity in a fallen world. This endeavor is grounded in the timeless truths of Scripture and is vital to the spiritual health and maturity of every believer.

Cultivating a Balanced and Reasoned Approach to Life

In the pursuit of a Christian life that honors God, it is imperative that believers cultivate a balanced and reasoned approach. This is not a call to cold logic or impersonal rationality, but rather an invitation to harmonize one's life with the will and wisdom of God as revealed in the Scriptures. The call to be sound in mind, as taught in the Bible, is not merely about intellectual assent but involves the whole person—emotions, will, and intellect—brought under the Lordship of Christ.

The Imperative of Scriptural Engagement

Central to developing a balanced and reasoned mindset is the regular and thoughtful engagement with the Word of God. The Scriptures, written in Hebrew, Aramaic, and Greek, offer not just a set of rules, but a living and active discourse (Hebrews 4:12). Engaging with the original languages, like exploring the nuances of *agape* (ἀγάπη) for love or *eirene* (εἰρήνη) for peace, can deepen understanding and appreciation for the biblical message.

Reason and Emotion in Harmony

In the Hebrew conception, the heart (*leb* in Hebrew) is not just the seat of emotions but also of thought and will. Therefore, a balanced approach does not deny emotions but seeks to understand them in light of scriptural truth. The Psalms often exhibit this harmony, with the psalmists pouring out their hearts before God while also reaffirming their trust in His promises and character.

39

Wisdom and Discernment

The biblical idea of wisdom, *chokmah* in Hebrew and *sophia* in Greek, transcends mere knowledge. It entails a practical application of truth to life's circumstances. James 1:5 encourages believers to seek wisdom from God, who gives generously. A reasoned approach to life weighs the transient against the eternal, discerning the best course of action based on scriptural principles.

The Mind of Christ as a Model

Paul's exhortation in Philippians 2:5 to have the mind of Christ (*phroneo* Christou) is about adopting Christ's outlook and values. This mind is characterized by humility, selflessness, and obedience to God's will. When faced with decisions, a balanced Christian mind asks, "What aligns with the character and teachings of Jesus?"

The Renewal of the Mind

The apostle Paul's command in Romans 12:2 to be transformed by the renewal of the mind is about an ongoing process, not a one-time event. This transformation (*metanoia* in Greek) involves a complete change in how one views the world, informed by Scripture rather than the prevailing culture. The mind, *nous* in Greek, becomes the battleground where truth contends with error.

The Conscience and Its Nurturing

The conscience, a God-given internal compass, must be informed and shaped by the truth of God's Word. Like a muscle that strengthens with use, the conscience becomes more sensitive and effective as it is trained by constant reference to biblical teachings. Paul discusses this in 1 Timothy 1:5, where the aim of the charge is love that issues from a pure heart and a good conscience and sincere faith.

The Community of Believers as a Resource

A reasoned approach to life is not meant to be developed in isolation. Believers are called to be of one mind with one another, echoing the New Testament Greek term *homothumadon* (ὁμοθυμαδόν), which signifies a harmonious togetherness. This unity of mind is fostered as believers study, worship, and serve together, offering counsel and encouragement rooted in Scripture.

Resistance to Worldly Philosophies

The balanced Christian mind must stand guard against the insidious infiltration of worldly philosophies that set themselves up against the knowledge of God (2 Corinthians 10:5). The term *logismos* (λογισμός) here refers to reasoning or arguments that must be brought into captivity to Christ. This does not mean rejecting all secular knowledge, but it does mean scrutinizing all thoughts and ideas through the lens of biblical truth.

The Role of Prayer in Mental Balance

Prayer is the lifeline that connects the believer to God, and it plays a crucial role in maintaining a balanced and reasoned life. In prayer, Christians express their dependence on God, seek His guidance, and align their will with His. The Greek word for prayer, *proseuche* (προσευχή), indicates not just a request for needs but a turning of the mind towards God.

The Practice of Moderation

The Greek term *enkrateia* (ἐγκράτεια), often translated as self-control or temperance, speaks to the practice of moderation. It is part of the fruit of the Spirit listed in Galatians 5:23. A sound mind exercises control over impulses and desires, choosing instead actions that are beneficial and edifying.

Edward D. Andrews

Embracing Suffering as a Path to Maturity

Understanding that God allows suffering for various reasons, including the development of Christian character, is part of a balanced mindset. This is not to glorify suffering in itself but to recognize its potential to produce endurance, character, and hope (Romans 5:3-4), shaping the believer into the likeness of Christ.

Integration of Faith and Daily Living

Finally, a balanced and reasoned approach to life requires the integration of faith into every aspect of daily living. It is not enough to be sound in mind in matters of doctrine; this soundness must permeate relationships, work, and even leisure, reflecting the holistic nature of the biblical teaching on soundness of mind. The apostle John's third letter, verse 2, expresses this well, wishing for the recipient's well-being just as his soul is well.

In conclusion, cultivating a balanced and reasoned approach to life involves a deep engagement with Scripture, an embrace of both reason and emotion, a reliance on prayer and community, and a vigilant stance against worldly philosophies. It is a comprehensive process, integrating faith with every area of life, always seeking to reflect the mind of Christ and the wisdom of God.

Protecting Our Minds From Corrupting Influences

In the journey of faith, the minds of Christians are the locus of a profound battle—a battle that entails not merely the acquisition of knowledge but the very essence of what it means to align with the will and purposes of God. The struggle for the Christian mind is not against flesh and blood but against corrupting influences that can distort, damage, and ultimately destroy the believer's capacity to reflect the image of Christ within the world. The Scriptures are clear: the heart of the discerning acquires knowledge, for the ears of the wise seek it out (Proverbs 18:15). But this seeking is not without its challenges, for

42

the mind is a battlefield upon which the forces of darkness often wage war.

The apostle Paul was acutely aware of the dangers posed by false ideologies and errant philosophies that sought to infiltrate the early Church. He warned the Colossians to see to it that no one takes them captive through hollow and deceptive philosophy, which depends on human tradition and the elemental spiritual forces of this world rather than on Christ (Colossians 2:8). This deceptive philosophy (*philosophia*) refers to a love or pursuit of wisdom that is antithetical to the wisdom found in Christ. It speaks of systems of thought that, while perhaps alluring and intellectually satisfying on a superficial level, are fundamentally at odds with the truth of the gospel.

The challenge for the believer, then, is manifold. Firstly, there is the need to recognize the inherent susceptibility of the human mind to deception. This susceptibility is rooted in the Fall, with the prophet Jeremiah reminding us that the heart is deceitful above all things, and desperately sick; who can understand it? (Jeremiah 17:9). This treachery of the heart (*lev*) reflects an inner corruption that only the truth of God can remedy.

Secondly, Christians must be vigilant in guarding their minds against the barrage of ungodly messages and influences that characterize much of contemporary society. The visual and narrative media that pervade our culture are often carriers of ideologies that subtly and not-so-subtly express worldviews and moral perspectives at odds with Scripture. From the normalization of lust and material greed to the valorization of pride and self-centeredness, these messages are powerful forces that can shape desires, attitudes, and ultimately, behaviors.

The apostle Paul's admonition to the Ephesians is relevant here: Let no one deceive you with empty words, for because of such things God's wrath comes on those who are disobedient (Ephesians 5:6). The term for empty words (*kenois logois*) implies messages devoid of spiritual and moral substance, seductive in their appeal but hollow at the core. Christians are to discern these messages and resist their influence, not merely through avoidance but through the cultivation of a mind deeply rooted in Scripture.

This leads to the third imperative: the positive fortification of the mind with divine truth. Paul exhorts believers to be transformed by the renewal of their minds (Romans 12:2). The Greek term for transformed (*metamorphoo*) denotes a profound change, akin to the metamorphosis of a caterpillar into a butterfly. This transformation is not a passive process but an active pursuit of God's will, discerning what is good, acceptable, and perfect.

Renewal of the mind (*anakainosis tou noos*) involves a resolute turning away from patterns of thought and reasoning that are aligned with the old nature—the *sarx*, as Paul refers to it, the fleshly or sinful aspect of humanity—and a turning toward the mind of Christ (*nous Christou*). This mind of Christ is characterized by humility, obedience to God, and a sacrificial love for others. It is a mind steeped in the Scriptures, able to "demolish arguments and every pretension that sets itself up against the knowledge of God" (2 Corinthians 10:5).

A critical aspect of this protective strategy is the conscious cultivation of a good conscience. The conscience (*suneidesis*) serves as a moral compass, shaped and informed by God's Word. When heeded and trained by consistent application of biblical truth, the conscience becomes a reliable guide. However, if ignored or repeatedly violated, the conscience can become seared—as if cauterized—losing its sensitivity to the promptings of the Holy Spirit as conveyed through the Scriptures.

Additionally, believers are encouraged to nurture a lowliness of mind (*tapeinophrosyne*), an attitude that esteems others more highly than oneself, following the example of Christ Jesus who, though he was in the form of God, did not count equality with God a thing to be grasped, but emptied himself (Philippians 2:3-7). This humble mindset is crucial in maintaining a posture of teachability and openness to correction from the Word of God and from fellow believers.

The renewal of the mind is a community project as well. Christians are called to be of the same mind (*auto phronein*), to be united in thought and purpose with fellow believers. This unity of mind is not the imposition of uniformity but the harmony that arises from shared commitment to Christ and to the truths of Scripture. It is a mind that is attuned to the *logos* of God—the Word, through which the worlds were framed and by which all things hold together.

In conclusion, protecting our minds from corrupting influences is an active, vigilant, and communal pursuit. It involves recognizing our vulnerability to deception, discerning and resisting ungodly influences, renewing our minds through immersion in God's Word, cultivating a good conscience, embracing humility, and fostering unity of mind with other believers. It is through these practices that Christians can stand firm in the truth and wield the sword of the Spirit, which is the Word of God, effectively in the battle for the mind.

Practical Steps to Developing a Sound Mind

In the ongoing battle for the Christian mind, the quest for *sophrosyne*—a sound mind or soundness of mind—is both a defensive and an offensive strategy against the wiles of the adversary. Developing a sound mind is not merely a passive state of mental health but an active pursuit of divine wisdom and understanding, which aligns the believer's thought life with the will of Jehovah. This alignment requires deliberate and disciplined effort, as the mind is not inherently sound but is bent towards evil and deception, as highlighted by the prophet Jeremiah when he noted the treacherous heart of humanity (Jeremiah 17:9). Paul also recognized this battle, emphasizing that our weapons are not carnal but mighty in God for pulling down strongholds (2 Corinthians 10:4).

Cultivating Biblical Knowledge

The foundational step to developing a sound mind is the cultivation of biblical knowledge. This is not simply an accumulation of facts but a deep, meditative engagement with the *logos*—the Word of God. As the psalmist wrote, "Your word is a lamp to my feet and a light to my path" (Psalm 119:105). Knowledge of the Scriptures is essential for discerning truth from error, righteousness from wickedness. The *dianoia*, or the mind, is to be saturated with the teachings of Jesus and the apostles, allowing the Word to dwell richly within us (Colossians 3:16). This rich dwelling is not merely intellectual assent but involves a deep-seated commitment to the truths of Scripture, embracing them as the ultimate reality that governs life and conduct.

Sharpening Discernment

With a foundation of biblical knowledge, discernment becomes the lens through which a Christian views the world. The Greek term *diakrisis* speaks to the ability to judge well, to differentiate between spirits of truth and error (1 Corinthians 12:10). A sound mind is thus characterized by *diakrisis*, the sharpened ability to make judgments based on the Word of God. For instance, when encountering various philosophies or lifestyles, a person with a sound mind tests them against biblical teachings, recognizing what aligns with godly wisdom and what is rooted in the deceit of the adversary.

Renewing the Mind

Paul's imperative to the Romans to be transformed by the renewing of their minds (*nous*) highlights the dynamic and ongoing nature of achieving sound-mindedness (Romans 12:2). Renewal suggests a continual process, where old, sinful patterns of thought are replaced by thoughts that are in harmony with the mind of Christ (*nous Christou*). This renewal is a work of the Spirit through the Word, not an indwelling presence but a guiding force as one internalizes and applies Scripture to every aspect of life.

Strengthening the Conscience

A Christian's conscience (*suneidesis*) is the inner faculty that accuses or excuses actions and attitudes (Romans 2:15). To be sound in mind, one must have a strong, biblically informed conscience. This requires regular feeding on the Word, which acts as a sharp sword to discern thoughts and intentions of the heart (Hebrews 4:12). A healthy conscience is sensitive to the Spirit's guidance through God's Word, prompting the believer toward righteousness and away from sin. If neglected, the conscience can become seared (*kauteriazo*), losing its effectiveness and leading one into spiritual peril.

Embracing the Mind of Christ

To possess the mind of Christ is to adopt a posture of humility and obedience, as exemplified by Jesus himself (Philippians 2:5-8). This *phronema* of Christ implies a mindset that prioritizes the interests of Jehovah and others above personal ambition or desire. It involves a lowliness of mind (*tapeinophrosyne*), a recognition of one's limitations, and a deep dependence on Jehovah for wisdom and strength.

Unifying with Fellow Believers

Unity of mind (*homophron*) among believers is not merely an ideal but a practical reality that must be pursued (1 Peter 3:8). As members of one body, Christians are to have the same care for one another, rejoicing and suffering together (1 Corinthians 12:25-26). This unity is not uniformity of thought but a harmonious diversity where each member contributes their gifts and insights under the headship of Christ, upholding the same core truths of the faith.

Engaging in Spiritual Warfare

Finally, developing a sound mind includes recognizing the spiritual nature of the battle we face. Paul spoke of our warfare not being carnal but mighty in God for the pulling down of strongholds (2 Corinthians 10:4). These strongholds are ideologies, arguments, and pretensions that set themselves up against the knowledge of Jehovah. To combat these, one must wield the *machaira* of the Spirit, the Word of God, with precision and authority, demolishing these strongholds and taking every thought captive to obey Christ.

In practical terms, this means that believers must be vigilant in prayer, consistent in studying and meditating on the Scriptures, and committed to living out their faith in community with other believers. The cultivation of a sound mind is a journey that requires persistence, the embrace of biblical truth, and the forsaking of worldly wisdom. Through these practical steps, Christians can develop minds that are sound, alert, and fully equipped for every good work that Jehovah has prepared in advance for us to do (Ephesians 2:10).

CHAPTER 4 What Is the Mind of Christ?

Exploring the Attitudes and Thoughts of Christ

The *nous Christou,* or the mind of Christ, encapsulates the attitudes and thoughts that were present in Jesus during His earthly ministry. These are not merely cognitive beliefs but are deeply entrenched perspectives and inclinations that shaped His actions and teachings. Understanding the mind of Christ is foundational for Christians who seek to align their own thinking with that of their Savior.

The Humility of Christ

One of the hallmark attitudes of Christ was His humility. The Greek term *tapeinophrosyne* describes this as lowliness of mind, which is evident in Jesus' willingness to empty Himself and take on the form of a servant (Philippians 2:7). This humility was not a passive disposition but an active stance that led Jesus to associate with those who were marginalized and deemed unimportant by society. For instance, He conversed with the Samaritan woman at the well (John 4:7-26), touched lepers whom others avoided (Matthew 8:3), and welcomed little children when the disciples saw them as a nuisance (Mark 10:13-16). These actions were radical in a culture that prized honor and status, showcasing that the mind of Christ values individuals not based on societal standing but on their inherent worth as persons created in the image of Jehovah.

Obedience to Jehovah's Will

The attitude of Christ was one of complete obedience to Jehovah's will. Jesus' prayer in the garden of Gethsemane, "*not as I will, but as you will*" (Matthew 26:39), demonstrates His submission to the

Father's plan, even unto death. Obedience for Christ was not a burdensome duty but a natural outflow of His love for the Father and commitment to the salvation of humanity. This obedience is seen in His meticulous fulfillment of Old Testament prophecies and His adherence to Jehovah's commands throughout His life.

Love and Compassion

The Greek word *agape*, often used to describe the love of Christ, signifies a self-sacrificing kind of love that is active and volitional. Jesus' compassion for the multitudes who were "harassed and helpless, like sheep without a shepherd" (Matthew 9:36) moved Him to teach, heal, and feed them. His miracles were not mere displays of power (*dunamis*) but manifestations of deep compassion and concern for the physical and spiritual well-being of the people. The feeding of the 5000, healing of the sick, and raising of the dead were all actions prompted by a loving disposition that saw beyond the immediate needs to the deeper spiritual hunger and pain.

Purity and Holiness

Christ's mind was characterized by purity and holiness, without the corruption that plagues human thought. The term *hagios* in Greek refers to being set apart, and Jesus was set apart from sinners, as He was without sin (Hebrews 7:26). His interactions were untainted by the deceptive and selfish motivations that often drive human behavior. When Jesus drove out the money changers from the temple, His zeal for Jehovah's house was clear; His actions were not out of impulsive anger but out of a desire to purify worship from commercial exploitation (John 2:13-17).

Wisdom and Understanding

Wisdom (*sophia*) in biblical terms is the skillful living according to Jehovah's standards, and understanding (*synesis*) is the comprehension of how to apply this wisdom in various circumstances. Jesus, even as a young boy, was found in the temple courts, "sitting among the teachers, listening to them and asking them questions" (Luke 2:46). His understanding astonished the teachers, and His wisdom, as He grew, was recognized by all (Luke 2:52). The Sermon on the Mount (Matthew 5–7) reflects this profound wisdom, as Jesus provided deep insights into the nature of the Kingdom of Heaven and the true intent behind Jehovah's laws.

Suffering and Endurance

The mind of Christ is also a mind acquainted with suffering (*pathema*) and characterized by endurance (*hypomone*). He was a man of sorrows, familiar with pain (Isaiah 53:3). Jesus endured hostility and rejection without retaliation, entrusting Himself to Jehovah who judges justly (1 Peter 2:23). His endurance on the cross, despising its shame for the joy set before Him, showcases the resolve and strength of the mind of Christ (Hebrews 12:2).

Forgiveness and Mercy

The thoughts and attitudes of Christ are epitomized in His words from the cross, "Father, forgive them, for they do not know what they are doing" (Luke 23:34). The Greek word for forgiveness, *aphesis*, conveys a release or letting go, which Jesus embodied even towards those who crucified Him. This forgiveness was not a mere utterance but a testament to the merciful heart (*splagchnon*) of Christ that extends grace even to the undeserving.

In the practical application of these principles, Christians are called to mirror these attitudes of Christ in their own lives. This is not achieved by sheer willpower but through the transformative work of the Spirit through the Word of God, as they continually immerse themselves in the Scriptures, allowing the Holy Spirit to use the Word to mold their thinking and actions. The mind of Christ is thus the ideal, the pattern, and the guiding principle for every believer seeking to live a life that honors Jehovah and reflects the character of Jesus.

The Humility and Obedience of Christ as Our Model

The concept of humility in the life of Jesus Christ is not just a peripheral character trait but is central to understanding His incarnation, ministry, and atoning work. In Philippians 2:5-8, Paul speaks of Jesus' *kenosis* (κένωσις), a self-emptying where Christ, though in the form of God, did not count equality with God a thing to be grasped, but emptied Himself, taking the form of a servant, being born in the likeness of men. This passage reveals the profound mystery of divine humility—God Almighty, willing to step into the bounds of human limitation, not in pomp and glory, but in lowliness and servitude.

Jesus' birth in a manger is emblematic of this humility. He was born not among royalty or in a palace, but in a stable—a place for animals. The infinite Word (λόγος) became flesh and dwelt among us (John 1:14), starting His human journey in the most humble of circumstances. Jesus did not use His divine status for His own advantage; rather, He relinquished the privileges it afforded to serve others.

In *tapeinophrosyne* (ταπεινοφροσύνη), or humility, there is a mindset that esteems others above oneself (Philippians 2:3). Jesus' interactions with tax collectors, sinners, and those on the fringes of society exemplified this. He washed the feet of His disciples, a task reserved for the lowest of servants, to demonstrate that the greatest in the Kingdom is the one who serves (John 13:14-15). This act was a concrete demonstration of humility, subverting the expectations of His followers who anticipated a messianic kingdom of power and conquest. Instead, He taught them that true greatness is not found in lordship but in servanthood.

The obedience (*hypakoē*, ὑπακοή) of Christ is another dimension that demands our attention. This obedience is not a begrudging acquiescence but a loving submission to Jehovah's will. It is a hallmark of His earthly ministry. Christ's obedience was prophesied in the Old Testament, where the suffering servant would be obedient even unto death (Isaiah 53). His life was a fulfillment of this prophetic obedience.

Throughout the Gospels, we observe Jesus' consistent submission to the Father's will. When facing the horrors of the crucifixion, His prayer in Gethsemane, *"not my will, but yours, be done"* (Luke 22:42), encapsulated the essence of His obedience. It was not without struggle or the absence of distress; His sweat was like drops of blood falling to the ground (Luke 22:44). Yet, His resolve did not waver.

In Jesus' obedience unto death, even death on a cross (Philippians 2:8), we find a model of steadfast commitment to Jehovah's purposes. It was through this obedience that salvation was extended to humanity. It was not through glorious triumph but through the ignominy and apparent defeat of the cross that Jesus conquered sin and death. He became obedient to the point of death, bearing the weight of sin and its consequences in a way no other could.

The humility and obedience of Christ also serve as a framework for understanding the Christian life. They are not just principles to admire but standards to emulate. As believers, the call is to a life of humility, not seeking personal glory but looking to the interests of others (Philippians 2:4), and to a life of obedience, following Jehovah's directives even when they lead us into difficult and painful experiences. This dual emphasis on humility and obedience acts as a bulwark against the pride and self-will that so often characterize human nature.

Christ's *agape* (ἀγάπη) love, a self-sacrificial love that seeks the good of the other above oneself, was both the motive and the method of His humility and obedience. This love was not abstract or detached; it was profoundly relational and incarnational, expressed in the grit and grind of everyday life. The *logos* (λόγος) of love became flesh in Jesus Christ and dwelt among us, providing an exemplar of the God-kind of love that believers are called to embody.

Moreover, the humility and obedience of Christ are not just moral exemplars; they are transformative forces. In embracing the mind of Christ, believers are invited to experience a metamorphosis, a renewing of their minds (Romans 12:2), that aligns their thoughts and actions with the divine pattern revealed in Jesus. It is not through the indwelling of the Holy Spirit as a separate entity but through the living and active Word of God that this transformation occurs. The Scriptures, inspired by the Holy Spirit, are the believer's guide to adopting the mind of Christ. They provide the *dunamis* (δύναμις), the power to demolish strongholds of erroneous thinking and to cultivate a Christ-like mindset.

In summary, the humility and obedience of Christ are far more than ethical ideals; they are the very essence of His identity and mission, which believers are called to imitate. They are not passive qualities but dynamic and powerful attributes that, when embraced, will mold a believer's character and conduct to reflect the likeness of Christ, thereby engaging in the battle for the Christian mind with the formidable weapons of Christ's own attitudes and actions.

Applying the Mind of Christ in Everyday Life

The endeavor to apply the mind of Christ in the daily life of a believer is a transformative journey that requires both understanding and action. It involves seeing the world through the lens of Jesus' teachings and character, aligning one's thoughts and behaviors with biblical principles, and manifesting the fruits of such a transformation in every aspect of life.

Cultivating a Christ-Centric Perspective

To possess the mind of Christ is to adopt a perspective that is deeply rooted in scriptural truth. This requires the believer to immerse themselves in the Scriptures, allowing the words of God to inform their worldview. The Greek term *nous* (νοῦς), often translated as "mind," refers to the faculty of understanding, perception, and thought. It is this *nous* that must be conformed to Christ's own through deliberate and continuous study of God's Word.

Embracing Biblical Truths in Decision Making

In everyday decisions, from the mundane to the significant, applying the mind of Christ means asking oneself what Jesus would prioritize according to Scripture. This calls for a *sunesis* (σύνεσις), which means an insightful understanding or practical wisdom that comes from God. Every choice made should reflect the principles Jesus lived by—love, humility, integrity, and obedience to Jehovah.

Transforming Interpersonal Relationships

The relational aspect of a Christian's life must also exhibit the mind of Christ. Interactions with family, friends, and even strangers should be characterized by *agape* (ἀγάπη), the selfless love that Jesus demonstrated. Believers are to love others as themselves, showing patience, kindness, and forgiveness. This love is not a mere emotion but an active choice that mirrors the compassion Christ showed to all.

Confronting Challenges with Christ-Like Resilience

When faced with trials and temptations, the believer is equipped to stand firm using the example of Christ's own perseverance. Just as Jesus overcame the world's tribulations, so too are Christians called to endure, relying not on their own strength but on the *dunamis* (δύναμις) provided by adherence to biblical teachings.

Developing a Lowly Mind through Service

Service is a practical expression of humility, a core attribute of the mind of Christ. Engaging in acts of service, whether within the church or in the broader community, fosters a *tapeinophrosyne* (ταπεινοφροσύνη), a modesty or lowliness of mind that esteems others more highly than oneself. Service is not for self-glorification but is a reflection of Jesus' own servant-heartedness.

Pursuing Unity in the Body of Christ

Unity within the Christian congregation is a testament to the collective pursuit of the mind of Christ. The Greek term *homothymadon* (ὁμοθυμαδόν), meaning with one accord or mind, exemplifies the early believers' unity. Today, Christians strive for this same unity by promoting peace, encouraging one another, and upholding sound doctrine.

Renewing the Mind Daily

The mind of Christ is not a static acquisition but a dynamic process. The daily renewal of the mind, as instructed in Romans 12:2, involves a persistent effort to reject worldly patterns and to embrace spiritual discernment. It means becoming so acquainted with the Scriptures that biblical responses become an instinctive outflow of the believer's regenerated heart.

Overcoming Evil with Good

The propensity of the human heart toward evil is an ever-present challenge. Yet, with the mind of Christ, believers are equipped to overcome evil with good. This is not a passive resignation but an active engagement in doing what is right in the sight of Jehovah, as Jesus did, even in the face of opposition.

Living as Light in a Darkened World

Lastly, to apply the mind of Christ in everyday life means to be a light in a world shrouded in spiritual darkness. It involves not only avoiding the unfruitful works of darkness but also exposing them, as Jesus did, with the light of truth and righteousness.

In conclusion, the application of the mind of Christ in everyday life is an all-encompassing commitment. It is to view the world through the same lens as Jesus, making decisions in line with His teachings, transforming relationships through His love, confronting challenges with His resilience, serving with His humility, promoting unity with His singleness of purpose, renewing the mind with His focus on spiritual things, overcoming evil with His goodness, and illuminating the darkness with His truth. This is the life to which all believers are called—a life that reflects the mind of Christ in thought, word, and deed.

The Mind of Christ and Our Relationship with Others

In discussing the mind of Christ, it is imperative to consider the implications it has on our relationships with others. The Scriptures provide a clear template on how this divine perspective shapes and directs our interactions, attitudes, and behaviors towards our fellow human beings.

Interpersonal Dynamics Rooted in Agape Love

The mind of Christ brings to the forefront the Greek concept of *agape* (ἀγάπη), which embodies the idea of selfless, sacrificial love that acts in the best interest of others. This love transcends mere feelings and encompasses a deliberate choice, a commitment to embody the kind of love Jesus demonstrated. In our relationships, this means that actions, words, and decisions are to be saturated with this love, influencing how we address conflict, how we speak about and to each other, and how we prioritize the needs of others.

Humility as a Relational Keystone

Jesus' example teaches that *tapeinophrosyne* (ταπεινοφροσύνη), humility of mind, is not a sign of weakness but of great strength. This humility allows us to value others above ourselves, not looking to our own interests but to the interests of others as exemplified in Philippians 2:3-4. It challenges the believer to listen more than they speak, to serve rather than be served, and to admit wrongdoing and seek forgiveness when necessary.

The Principle of Forgiveness

Central to the mind of Christ is the principle of forgiveness, as embodied in the Lord's Prayer. The call to forgive *echarizomai* (ἐχαρίζομαι), to graciously give pardon, is a reflection of the undeserved forgiveness we have received from God. In our relationships, this means actively and continually forgiving those who wrong us, and seeking reconciliation whenever possible, reflecting the reconciliatory nature of Christ's work on the cross.

Building Up One Another in Truth and Love

The mind of Christ influences believers to use their words and actions to edify *oikodome* (οἰκοδομή), to build up the house, that is, the body of believers. This building up is done in truth and love, encouraging and strengthening one another in faith. In practical terms, this means offering encouragement, speaking truthfully but with kindness, and looking for ways to support each other's growth in Christlikeness.

Unity and Peace as Reflections of Christ

Christ's mind prioritizes unity and peace among believers. The Greek term *homothymadon* (ὁμοθυμαδόν) describes a harmony of mind and heart. This unity is not merely the absence of conflict but is a positive peace *eirene* (εἰρήνη), that actively seeks the wellbeing and concord among believers, much like the early church in Acts, which was marked by a unity of purpose and love.

Addressing Sin with Redemptive Intent

With the mind of Christ, the believer approaches sin within the body not with condemnation but with the aim of restoration. This reflects the principle found in Galatians 6:1 where believers are instructed to restore someone in a spirit of gentleness. This restorative approach is a careful balance of upholding the truth of Scripture while seeking to bring the errant individual back into fellowship with God and the community of faith.

Overcoming Evil with Good

Emulating the mind of Christ means repaying evil with good, as commanded in Romans 12:21. This counter-cultural response reflects a heart that trusts in God's sovereign justice and refuses to be overcome by the evil in the world. It involves proactive goodness that

57

seeks to demonstrate the transformative power of Christ's love in response to hatred, malice, and injustice.

To walk with the mind of Christ in our relationships is a comprehensive endeavor that reaches into every interaction. It is a radical departure from the self-centered mindset of the world and a journey towards embodying the love, humility, forgiveness, truth, unity, and redemptive spirit of Jesus. As we draw closer to the heart of God through His Word, we are continuously transformed, and our relationships become a vivid demonstration of the Gospel at work in our lives. Through these relationships, the mind of Christ becomes visible and tangible to a world in desperate need of His love and truth.

CHAPTER 5 The Battle for the Christian Mind

Recognizing the Warfare: Spiritual Versus Worldly Thinking

In the landscape of the Christian mind, there exists a continuous battle between spiritual wisdom and worldly reasoning. Understanding this conflict is crucial for believers who are called to develop a mindset that reflects the character and will of Jehovah rather than the pattern of this world.

The Contrast Between Flesh and Spirit

The Scriptures delineate a stark contrast between the *sarx* (σάρξ), the flesh, which pertains to a sinful nature, and the *pneuma* (πνεῦμα), the spirit, which should be guided by God's Word. Worldly thinking, which emanates from the flesh, is characterized by self-centeredness, materialism, and moral relativism. It operates under the influence of the "god of this system of things," as the apostle Paul describes in 2 Corinthians 4:4, which refers to Satan's control over the current sinful world. Spiritual thinking, however, seeks to align with divine principles, valuing what Jehovah values and discerning matters from an eternal perspective.

The Danger of the World's Philosophy

The Apostle Paul warns of the deceptive philosophy that comes from human tradition and the basic principles of the world rather than from Christ (Colossians 2:8). This worldly philosophy is steeped in pride and rebellion against God's authority, promoting ideas that may appear wise but are fundamentally flawed because they lack the truth of God. Spiritual warfare, then, involves the rejection of these hollow

59

and deceptive philosophies and a steadfast adherence to the teachings of the Scriptures.

The Renewal of the Mind

The transformation of the believer's mind is a pivotal theme in the New Testament. In Romans 12:2, Paul urges believers not to conform to the pattern of this world but to be transformed by the renewing of the mind. This renewal is a *metanoia* (μετάνοια), a complete change of mind and heart toward God's will, leading to a life that is able to test and approve what God's will is—his good, pleasing, and perfect will.

The Deceitfulness of Sin

Sin has a corrupting effect on the mind. Hebrews 3:13 speaks of the deceitfulness of sin, which can harden the heart. A worldly mind is susceptible to rationalizing sin, diminishing its seriousness, and ultimately being desensitized to its destructive nature. Spiritual thinking, in contrast, recognizes the gravity of sin and the necessity of repentance and reliance on the redemptive work of Christ.

Cognitive Dissonance in the Christian Experience

Christians may experience cognitive dissonance when their actions do not align with their professed beliefs. This dissonance is a manifestation of the conflict between spiritual and worldly thinking. The apostle Paul's discussion in Romans 7 about doing what he does not want to do and not doing what he wants to do illustrates this inner conflict. To overcome this, believers must constantly immerse themselves in the Word of God, allowing it to correct and guide them.

The Weaponry of Our Warfare

Believers are equipped with spiritual weapons to demolish strongholds of wrong thinking. These strongholds can be ideologies, opinions, or any thought patterns that set themselves up against the knowledge of God. The divine power that demolishes these strongholds is found in the truth of God's Word, prayer, and the application of biblical principles in everyday life.

The Importance of Discernment

Discernment is a critical asset in the believer's arsenal. The Greek term *diakrisis* (διάκρισις) denotes the ability to judge well. In spiritual warfare, discernment enables Christians to distinguish between truth and error, between what is of God and what is of the world. This discernment is honed through a deep engagement with Scripture and the wisdom that comes from above, which James describes as pure, peace-loving, considerate, submissive, full of mercy and good fruit, impartial and sincere (James 3:17).

Victory Through Christ

The ultimate victory in the battle for the mind comes through Christ, who, through His death and resurrection, has disarmed the powers and authorities, making a public spectacle of them, triumphing over them by the cross (Colossians 2:15). The believer's task is to cling to this victory, steadfastly abiding in Christ, for apart from Him, we can do nothing (John 15:5).

Recognizing the warfare between spiritual and worldly thinking is paramount for the believer. It involves an active rejection of the fleshly mindsets and philosophies that are in opposition to God and a wholehearted embrace of spiritual wisdom as revealed in Scripture. As Christians, we are called to vigilant minds, hearts guarded by the peace of God which surpasses all understanding, and lives that display the transformative power of the mind of Christ. Through this spiritual battle, the believer is sanctified, and the mind is conformed more and more to the likeness of Jesus Christ, reflecting the glory of God to a world ensnared by the deception of the evil one.

Edward D. Andrews

Satan's Tactics in the Battle for Our Minds

In the grand narrative of God's Word, the mind is depicted as the strategic battleground where the forces of good and evil vie for control. Satan, the adversary, employs a plethora of cunning tactics to influence and, if possible, dominate the minds of believers. The Scriptures unveil various methods used by the evil one to derail humans from the path of righteousness and truth. Understanding these tactics is pivotal for the Christian who seeks to safeguard the mind against the deceptions of the "wicked one" (*ho ponēros*).

Distortion of Truth

Satan's first tactic recorded in Scripture is the distortion of truth, beginning with the insidious question posed to Eve, "Did God actually say...?" (Genesis 3:1). He plants seeds of doubt regarding Jehovah's Word, twisting and contorting it to suit his agenda. The Greek term *diastrephō* (διαστρέφω), meaning to distort or turn aside, exemplifies Satan's method of warping the divine message, causing individuals to question the veracity and integrity of God's commandments.

The Appeal to Fleshly Desires

The enticement of the flesh is a potent weapon in Satan's arsenal. He preys on human weaknesses, the *epithymia* (ἐπιθυμία), or strong desires, that can lead a person away from spiritual commitments (James 1:14). By appealing to these fleshly desires, Satan promotes a mindset that prioritizes immediate gratification over spiritual wellbeing, setting a snare for the unwary.

Exploitation of Human Weakness

The devil is described as prowling around like a roaring lion, seeking someone to devour (1 Peter 5:8). He meticulously exploits human vulnerabilities, those moments of *astheneia* (ἀσθένεια), or weakness, to advance his cause. This could manifest through

62

discouragement, fatigue, fear, or any other state that diminishes a believer's reliance on Jehovah and susceptibility to spiritual attack.

Propagation of Lies and False Doctrines

Satan is the father of lies (*pseudos* in Greek, John 8:44), and his legacy includes the propagation of false doctrines. These erroneous teachings are strategically designed to lead astray, to undermine faith, and to sow confusion and division among believers. He capitalizes on the human propensity for *itching ears*, an eagerness to hear something new and different, which can result in a departure from the sound doctrine of the Scriptures (2 Timothy 4:3-4).

Fomenting Doubt and Unbelief

A critical aspect of Satan's strategy is to foment doubt and unbelief, attacking the very foundation of a Christian's faith. He implants questions regarding Jehovah's goodness, sovereignty, and the reliability of His promises, intending to erode trust in God. The term *apistia* (ἀπιστία), or unbelief, marks the ultimate goal of Satan's tactic, leading individuals to question the core truths that anchor them to Christ.

The Use of Persecution and Fear

Satan often resorts to intimidation tactics, leveraging persecution and fear to compromise a believer's commitment to God. The *phobos* (φόβος), or fear that arises in the face of opposition, can be a powerful deterrent to maintaining a steadfast confession of faith. By inciting fear, the enemy seeks to weaken the resolve of Christians and to deter them from proclaiming the gospel boldly.

Creating Division and Strife

A divided house cannot stand, and Satan knows this well. He instigates *eris* (ἔρις), strife, and discord within the body of Christ to destabilize and weaken its collective witness. By amplifying misunderstandings, cultural differences, and personal grievances, Satan attempts to fracture the unity that should define the church.

Promoting Worldly Wisdom Over Divine Revelation

The wisdom of this world is folly to God (1 Corinthians 3:19). Satan promotes a system of thought that exalts human reasoning and *sophia* (σοφία), or wisdom, above divine revelation. He encourages a reliance on intellectual pride and self-sufficiency, which leads away from a dependent relationship with Jehovah and a humble submission to His will as revealed in the Scriptures.

Distracting from the Simplicity of Christ

One of Satan's subtle tactics is to draw believers away from the simplicity and purity of devotion to Christ (2 Corinthians 11:3). He introduces complexities, legalisms, and extrabiblical requirements that can burden and entangle a believer, distracting from the central focus on Christ as the sole mediator and redeemer.

Encouraging Worldly Success and Materialism

The lure of material success and the trappings of worldly wealth can be a distracting force. Satan tempted Jesus with all the kingdoms of the world and their glory (*doxa* in Greek, Matthew 4:8). He continues to use this temptation, suggesting that worldly achievement and accumulation are of ultimate importance, thereby diverting attention and devotion away from Jehovah.

To counteract these tactics, the Christian is called to be vigilant, to remain grounded in the truth of God's Word, and to be continually transformed by the renewal of the mind. This spiritual renewal is a defense against the mental onslaught of the evil one and essential for living a life pleasing to Jehovah. As believers clothe themselves with the full armor of God, they can stand firm against the schemes of the devil, holding fast to faith as a shield and the Word of God as the sword of the Spirit (Ephesians 6:11-17). The battle for the Christian mind is fierce, but with Jehovah's help and the guidance of His Spirit-inspired Word, victory is assured.

Arming Ourselves with the "Sword of the Spirit"

In the spiritual conflict that rages for dominion over the Christian mind, we are not left defenseless. The Apostle Paul delineates the panoply of God in Ephesians 6, and preeminent among these divine provisions is the "sword of the Spirit," which is the Word of God (*rhēma tou Theou*). This potent metaphor illustrates that our primary offensive weapon in this battle is Scripture itself, which is sharper than any two-edged sword (*machaira*), penetrating to the division of soul and of spirit (Hebrews 4:12). This chapter will unfold how to effectively wield this "sword" to safeguard our minds and repel the assaults of the enemy.

The "sword of the Spirit" is not a mere metaphor; it represents the dynamic and living words of God, which have the power (*dunamis*) to demolish the strongholds of false reasoning and to establish truth in the fortress of the mind. The Word of God carries the authority (*exousia*) of Jehovah Himself, for it is inspired—*theopneustos*, God-breathed (2 Timothy 3:16). Therefore, in arming ourselves, we must first and foremost cultivate a deep and abiding relationship with Scripture.

Imbibing the Scripture requires an intense, continual interaction with the text. This is not a superficial reading but a *meditatio*—a meditation wherein one ruminates on the Word, allowing it to percolate through the layers of the soul. David, the psalmist, exemplifies this practice when he declares, "I have stored up your word in my heart, that I might not sin against you" (Psalm 119:11). Storing up the Word in our hearts is a defensive tactic, ensuring that when temptations arise, the Spirit-inspired responses are ready at hand.

Understanding the Scripture goes beyond mere reading or memorization. It involves *synesis*, discernment, which the Holy Spirit provides through the text itself. The Bereans were commended for their noble character because they examined the Scriptures daily to see if what Paul said was true (Acts 17:11). They understood that discernment comes through diligent study, which in turn equips the believer to discern between good and evil (Hebrews 5:14).

Applying the Scripture is the thrust of wielding the "sword of the Spirit." It is not enough to know the Word; we must let it transform us. The Word of God is described as living and active, discerning the thoughts and intentions of the heart (Hebrews 4:12). This *energēs*, or effective work of the Word, is realized when it is applied to daily living. James exhorts believers to be doers of the Word, not hearers only, thereby avoiding self-deception (James 1:22).

Defending with Scripture involves utilizing the Word of God to refute false doctrines, heresies, and deceptions that pervade the world and sometimes infiltrate the church. When Jesus was tempted by Satan in the wilderness, His defense was threefold: "It is written" (Matthew 4:4,7,10). Each temptation was countered with a precise and applicable Scripture, demonstrating how well-armed He was with the "sword of the Spirit."

Proclaiming the Scripture is a vital aspect of the Christian's offensive strategy. Paul instructed Timothy to preach the Word, be ready in season and out of season, reprove, rebuke, and exhort with complete patience and teaching (2 Timothy 4:2). The proclamation of the Word is the means by which truth is broadcast and the minds of hearers are challenged and transformed.

Uniting through Scripture is a powerful defensive formation. When believers are united in the truth of the Word, they present a formidable front against the enemy's attempts to sow discord. The *homothumadon*, or being of one mind, in the early church was a source of their strength and unity (Acts 2:46).

In this battle for the mind, the Word of God is the believer's indomitable weapon. But it is not our skill or strength that makes this "sword" effective; it is the power of Jehovah working through His Word. The *rhēma tou Theou* is not a static text but the active voice of God speaking to us today. It is the very breath of God that sustains us, directs us, corrects us, and enables us to stand firm in the face of the enemy's attacks.

To wield the "sword of the Spirit" effectively, we must engage with the Word of God at a level that goes beyond intellectual assent. We must allow it to penetrate our hearts, to shape our thinking, and to direct our actions. This is the transformation that Paul speaks of in Romans 12:2, a metamorphosis of the mind that results in discerning the will of Jehovah. The battle for the Christian mind is relentless, but it is also one in which victory is assured, for "the word of our God will stand forever" (Isaiah 40:8). As we arm ourselves with the "sword of the Spirit," we align ourselves with the mind of Christ, ensuring that every thought is taken captive to obey Christ (2 Corinthians 10:5). This is not merely an individual endeavor but a collective calling for the body of Christ, for as we stand together, armed with the truth, we can resist the devil, and he will flee from us (James 4:7).

Strategies for Preserving a Christian Mindset in a Secular World

In the relentless surge of secularism, the Christian mind is often besieged by philosophies and ideologies at odds with the teachings of Scripture. The apostle Paul recognized this threat when he admonished believers to not be conformed to this world but to be transformed by the renewal of their mind (Romans 12:2). This transformation is not a passive occurrence but the result of deliberate and strategic engagement with the Spirit-inspired Word of God. The strategies that follow are designed to fortify the Christian mindset amidst a secular milieu.

Immersing in the Word of God

The foundational strategy for preserving a Christian mindset is to immerse oneself in the Word of God. David extolled the virtues of God's law, meditating on it day and night (Psalm 1:2). This meditation is more than a cursory reading; it is an *iyyun*, a deep and reflective study that allows the truth of the Scriptures to permeate every facet of our being. The Greek term *logos* encapsulates not only the spoken word but also the divine rationale behind it. It is the *logos* of God that must dwell richly in the believer, teaching and admonishing in all wisdom

(Colossians 3:16). By consistently feeding on the Scriptures, our minds are renewed, aligning our thoughts and purposes with those of Christ.

Engaging with the Original Languages

A deeper understanding of Scripture often comes from a direct engagement with the original languages—Hebrew and Greek. For instance, the Hebrew word *shalom* is often translated as "peace," but its semantic range extends to wholeness, completeness, and well-being. Engaging with this richer meaning can profoundly affect how one assimilates the concept of peace in the biblical context. Similarly, the Greek word *agape* describes a love that is selfless and sacrificial—far exceeding the English counterpart in depth. Encouraging believers to delve into these original terms enriches their scriptural understanding and anchors their mindset in the true essence of biblical teachings.

Cultivating a Discerning Spirit

The Christian mind must be sharpened to discern truth from deception. The Greek term *diakrisis* refers to the ability to distinguish and determine what is true. The writer of Hebrews commends those who by constant practice have trained their faculties of *sunesis*, or understanding, to distinguish good from evil (Hebrews 5:14). In a world brimming with information and opinions, discernment is a guardrail that keeps the Christian from veering off the path of truth. It requires a familiarity with Scripture so intimate that any foreign element is immediately recognizable.

Practicing the Presence of God

In cultivating a Christian mindset, one must live in constant acknowledgment of Jehovah's presence. This is not a mystical practice but a conscious realization that we live *coram Deo*—before the face of God. The Hebrew word *halakh* denotes one's manner of life, suggesting that walking in the presence of Jehovah involves a comprehensive pattern of behavior (Genesis 17:1). This awareness influences our decisions, shapes our thoughts, and enables us to view every aspect of life through the lens of Scripture.

Communing with Like-Minded Believers

The New Testament emphasizes the importance of *koinonia*, fellowship with other believers. This communion fosters a shared mindset that is grounded in the faith once for all delivered to the saints (Jude 1:3). It provides a support system where truths are affirmed, errors are corrected, and the individual mind is fortified through the collective wisdom of the body of Christ.

Conforming to the Image of Christ

The ultimate goal of preserving a Christian mindset is to conform to the image of Christ (*eikon Christou*). This involves a *morphosis*, a transformation that reshapes our mind and character to reflect Jesus' humility, obedience, and love. Paul spoke of having the mind of Christ (*nous Christou*), which requires us to adopt the same attitude of servitude and sacrifice that characterized His earthly ministry (Philippians 2:5-8).

Implementing Scriptural Principles in Everyday Decisions

The secular world often operates on principles at odds with Scripture. It is crucial, therefore, that believers implement scriptural principles in their everyday decisions. This implementation is not about legalistic adherence to rules but about applying the wisdom of God's Word to the varied circumstances of life. When faced with ethical dilemmas or moral choices, the Christian should ask, "What does the Scripture say?" (*Ti legi he graphe*; Romans 4:3), allowing the Word of God to guide their actions and decisions.

Utilizing Apologetics

Apologetics, the reasoned defense of the faith (*apologia*), equips the believer to counter the challenges posed by secular thought. It involves understanding the arguments for the Christian worldview and being able to communicate them effectively (1 Peter 3:15). Apologetics is not about winning arguments but about presenting the reasons for our hope with gentleness and respect, thereby influencing the secular mind with the credibility of the gospel.

Committing to Prayerful Dependence

Finally, the Christian mind is preserved by a commitment to prayerful dependence on Jehovah. The believer is exhorted to pray without ceasing (*adialeiptos proseuchesthai*; 1 Thessalonians 5:17), acknowledging that every breath and thought is sustained by God. Through prayer, the Christian expresses reliance on Jehovah, not as a mere ritual, but as a heartfelt recognition of His sovereignty and grace.

By implementing these strategies, the believer actively combats the influence of secularism. The battle for the Christian mind is indeed intense, but it is not fought in human strength. The power of God's Spirit, expressed through His inspired Word, equips believers to stand firm in a world that is often hostile to the truths of Scripture. In doing so, the Christian mindset is not only preserved but also strengthened and refined for the glory of Jehovah.

CHAPTER 6 Be Transformed by the Renewal of Our Mind

The Process of Transformation: How It Begins and Continues

Transformation in the Christian life is both a momentous event and a progressive journey, a remarkable blend of the immediate and the continuous. It commences with an encounter and perpetuates through a life of persistent change.

The Genesis of Transformation

The initiation of transformation is captured succinctly in the concept of *metanoia*, a Greek term that implies a profound change of mind (Matthew 3:8). This change is not merely an emotional experience; it is a volitional and rational response to the truth of the gospel. It involves a recognition of our innate propensity for error and rebellion as described in Genesis 6:5 and Jeremiah 17:9.

When one comes to Christ, there is an awakening, a spiritual *photismos* (enlightenment, 2 Corinthians 4:6) that propels the believer from the domain of darkness into the kingdom of light. This enlightenment, however, is not the culmination but the commencement of a lifelong process. The apostle Paul elucidates this when he implores believers to be transformed by the renewal of their mind (*nous*), stressing an ongoing metamorphosis (Romans 12:2).

Continuity Through Renewal

The continuance of transformation is an active pursuit, a conscious endeavor to align our *dianoia* (thinking, Matthew 22:37) with the mind of Christ. This pursuit is driven by the Spirit-inspired Word of God, which acts as a mirror reflecting the thoughts and intents of the heart (Hebrews 4:12). The continuous renewal of the mind is akin to the iterative refinement of silver, removing dross to reveal pure metal.

Embracing the Word with the Mind of Christ

The mind of Christ is characterized by *tapeinophrosyne* (humility, Philippians 2:5-8) and an unwavering commitment to the will of the Father. Acquiring this mindset involves saturating our consciousness with the Scriptures, allowing the *rhema* (spoken word) of God to reshape our thoughts and attitudes. As we meditate on the Word, our spiritual faculties are honed to discern truth from falsehood, just as the conscience is sharpened to be more sensitive to moral and spiritual nuances.

The Role of Conscience in Transformation

Our conscience, an intrinsic aspect of our *psyche* (soul), is designed to be a barometer of righteousness. In a fallen state, the conscience can be seared, rendering it ineffective (1 Timothy 4:2). But as we engage with Scripture, our conscience is educated and invigorated. This process, however, is not automatic; it requires the believer to act upon the biblical truths learned. The Christian's goal is to have a conscience aligned with God's standards, a *suneidesis* that is not stained by the corruption of the world.

Unity of Mind in the Body of Christ

Transformation extends beyond the individual to the collective mind of the church, the *ekklesia*. The New Testament emphasizes a *phronema* (mindset, Romans 8:5-6) that is shared among believers, a spiritual synchronicity that strengthens the collective witness of the church. This unity is rooted in humility and is expressed through a life of service and love. The apostle Peter speaks to this collective mindset, urging believers to be like-minded, sympathetic, and humble (1 Peter 3:8).

The Dynamics of Spiritual Warfare

Transformation involves the dynamics of spiritual warfare. The believer's mind is the battlefield where truths confront lies, and peace contends with chaos. Paul's exhortation to use our spiritual weaponry to demolish strongholds is an invocation to apply divine power— *dunamis*—against the fortifications of erroneous thought patterns (2 Corinthians 10:4). These strongholds are dismantled not through human effort but through the potency of God's truth.

The Necessity of Scriptural Embrace

Understanding Scripture is not a mere intellectual exercise; it is a holistic embrace of its truths. The terms *analogia* (2 Peter 1:20) and *epignosis* (full knowledge, 2 Peter 1:3) refer to a comprehensive and accurate comprehension of scriptural truths, coupled with a heartfelt acceptance. In 1 Corinthians 2:14, Paul addresses the natural person's incapacity to embrace the things of the Spirit of God. This incapacity is not an intellectual deficit but a spiritual one, where divine truths are dismissed as folly.

Ongoing Transformation Through Practical Living

Transformation is authenticated in practical living. The scriptural principles must be woven into the fabric of our daily decisions and interactions. As we apply the principles of Scripture, our thought processes are refined. When confronted with decisions, we are to ask ourselves not only what is lawful but also what is beneficial (*sumphero*, 1 Corinthians 10:23). In this, we exercise our renewed minds, demonstrating the transformative power of the gospel.

The process of transformation is indeed a complex one, involving an initial awakening and a continuous renewal of the mind. This renewal is realized through the embrace of scriptural truth, the education of the conscience, the unity of the church, and the demolition of spiritual strongholds. As we journey through life, our transformation becomes evident in our thoughts, words, and deeds, reflecting the image of Christ to a world in need of His light. This

73

Edward D. Andrews

transformative journey is a testimony to the power of God's Word and Spirit in the life of the believer, showcasing the profound impact of a mind continually surrendered to the Lord.

The Role of the Scriptures in Renewing Our Minds

In the quest for a renewed mind, a concept paramount in the life of a believer, the Scriptures serve as the divine conduit through which the *nous* (mind) is both enlightened and transformed. This transformative journey involves both the acquisition of knowledge and the embracing of this knowledge with conviction and practice. The Scriptures, viewed through the lens of the Historical-Grammatical method of interpretation, provide the objective framework for this mental renewal.

Scripture: The Mirror for the Mind

As the psalmist proclaims, "The law of Jehovah is perfect, reviving the soul" (Psalm 19:7), there is an intrinsic power within the Word of God to effect change. This change is not superficial but reaches into the very depths of the *psyche* (soul), which encompasses the entirety of one's being. When a believer engages with Scripture, it acts as a mirror reflecting their true spiritual condition, revealing thoughts and intentions often hidden from the conscious mind (Hebrews 4:12). This confrontation with truth initiates the process of renewal.

Knowledge to Embrace: The Epignosis of Truth

In acquiring knowledge, one is not merely to accumulate facts but to gain *epignosis*, a precise and correct knowledge that leads to recognition and acknowledgment of truth (Colossians 3:10). This knowledge transcends mere cognition and must be received with an openness to its implications. When Paul speaks to the Ephesians about the renewing of the mind, he uses the term *ananeoo*, signifying a qualitative renewal—a total makeover of the inner self, not just a superficial adjustment (Ephesians 4:23).

Internalizing Scripture: The Role of Meditation

The Hebrew concept of *hagah* (meditation, Joshua 1:8) involves a murmuring or speaking under one's breath, indicating an intimate and ongoing engagement with the text. The practice of *hagah* is an example of how one internalizes Scripture. As the believer meditates, the Word transitions from being external information to becoming an integral part of their value system and worldview. This meditation is not an emptying of the mind, as seen in some Eastern practices, but a filling of the mind with divine truth.

Shaping the Conscience with the Word

A Christian's conscience is the inner faculty that accuses or excuses one's actions (Romans 2:15). This *suneidesis* (conscience) must be calibrated by the truth of God's Word. As the believer consistently exposes their conscience to Scripture, it becomes more sensitive to righteousness and sin. The Holy Spirit, through the Word, provides guidance and conviction, leading to a mind that reflects the moral clarity and ethical resolve seen in Jesus Christ.

Unity in Thought through Scriptural Saturation

In the collective setting of the church, *homothumadon* (being of one mind, Acts 1:14) is an essential attribute of a unified body. This unity is fostered as individuals renew their minds through Scripture, leading to a shared mindset anchored in biblical truth. The shared values and beliefs, nurtured through a common commitment to the Word, result in a spiritual congruence that binds the members together in purpose and understanding.

Overcoming Spiritual Strongholds through Scriptural Truth

The believer's mind often faces strongholds—*ochuromata* (fortified arguments, 2 Corinthians 10:4)—which are resistant to the knowledge of God. The Word of God possesses the *dunamis* (power) to demolish these strongholds. The truth of Scripture confronts and overpowers the lies and deceptions that entrench themselves in human thinking. This confrontation is not violent but persuasive, a gentle yet relentless displacement of error with truth.

From Cognitive Assent to Spiritual Embrace

Understanding and embracing Scripture requires a movement from *gnosis* (knowledge) to *epignosis* (full knowledge). This full knowledge is characterized by a deep conviction that results in a transformation of behavior and disposition. When Paul discusses the natural person's reception of spiritual truths in 1 Corinthians 2:14, he is speaking of a spiritual embrace that goes beyond intellectual acknowledgment. The unbeliever rejects the truths of Scripture not due to a lack of intellectual capacity but due to a spiritual unwillingness to submit to its authority.

Transforming Beliefs into Actions

The ultimate evidence of a renewed mind is the application of biblical principles in everyday life. James emphasizes this when he encourages believers to be doers of the Word, and not hearers only (James 1:22). The internalization of Scripture must manifest in external behaviors; otherwise, the renewal of the mind remains incomplete. It involves an ongoing process of replacing former behaviors and habits with actions that are in harmony with scriptural mandates.

Renewal as an Act of Worship

Renewing the mind is not merely for personal edification but is an act of worship—a spiritual service. In presenting our bodies as a living sacrifice, the renewing of our mind according to Romans 12:1-2 is the logical *latreia* (service) expected of those who follow Christ. The renewed mind is, therefore, not an end in itself but a means to glorify Jehovah and reflect His character.

The role of the Scriptures in the renewal of the mind is foundational and multifaceted. It involves a deliberate engagement with the Word, an internalization that shapes conscience, a collective unity of thought, the overcoming of spiritual strongholds, and the transformation of belief into action. Through the Scriptures, believers are not only informed but transformed, not only educated but also enlivened, as they seek to fulfill the divine mandate to be transformed by the renewal of their minds. This process reflects a profound reverence for the Word of God as the authoritative source for thought and life, embodying a devotion that transcends mere intellectual assent and culminates in a life that is a testament to the transformative power of divine truth.

Examples of Transformation in the Lives of Biblical Figures

The transformative power of God's Word is vividly displayed in the lives of various individuals throughout the Scriptures. These transformations provide concrete examples of how the renewal of the mind according to the will of Jehovah is neither abstract nor theoretical but a powerful, practical reality. The narratives of these figures unfold the remarkable transitions from flawed, often profoundly misguided characters to exemplars of faith and obedience, demonstrating the profound impact of divine revelation on the human *nous* (mind).

Saul of Tarsus to Paul the Apostle: A Radical Metanoia

One of the most striking examples is Saul of Tarsus, a Pharisee who zealously persecuted the early Christians. His transformation began on the road to Damascus when he encountered the risen Christ (Acts 9:3-6). This event sparked a complete *metanoia* (change of mind), leading to his conversion and subsequent mission as Paul the Apostle. This intellectual and spiritual overhaul was so thorough that he became the foremost exponent of the faith he once tried to destroy, dedicating his life to the proclamation of the Gospel. His letters, saturated with rich theological truths, reflect a mind deeply renewed and anchored in the knowledge of Christ.

Peter: From Reckless Impulsiveness to Apostolic Solidity

Simon Peter's transformation was a progressive journey marked by moments of recklessness, impulsiveness, and even failure. Yet, under the tutelage of Jesus and through the crucible of personal setbacks, Peter's *dianoia* (thinking) was reshaped. After his denial of Christ (Matthew 26:69-75) and subsequent restoration (John 21:15-19), Peter emerged as a pillar in the early church, boldly proclaiming the message he once feared to associate with. His epistles reflect a mature understanding of suffering, divine election, and the holy conduct required of believers.

Mary Magdalene: From Demonic Oppression to Devoted Follower

Mary Magdalene's life exemplifies the liberating power of Christ's ministry. She was delivered from seven demons (Luke 8:2), symbolizing a complete transformation from bondage to freedom. Her subsequent devotion to Christ, even to the foot of the cross and beyond as the first to witness the resurrection (John 20:1, 11-18), illustrates the profound impact of Jesus' healing on her *psyche* (soul). She embodies the paradigm of one whose mind and life were entirely renewed by her encounter with the Savior.

John: From Son of Thunder to Apostle of Love

John the Apostle, initially known as a 'Son of Thunder' (Mark 3:17), underwent a notable transformation in his disposition. Early in his discipleship, John exhibited a temperament marked by zealotry and a desire for retribution (Luke 9:54). However, through the teachings of Jesus and the intimate experiences shared with Him, John's character was softened, his *phronēma* (mindset) was renewed, and he became known for his emphasis on love, as profoundly expressed in his epistles. His writings encapsulate the essence of God as love (1 John 4:8) and the believer's call to embody this divine love.

Nebuchadnezzar: From Imperial Arrogance to Divine Acknowledgment

A transformation of a different order is seen in Nebuchadnezzar, the Babylonian king whose *ruach* (spirit) was humbled after experiencing a period of insanity for his pride (Daniel 4:33). Upon his restoration, he acknowledged the sovereignty of the Most High (Daniel 4:34-37). His transformation, from a ruler who reveled in his own glory to one who recognized Jehovah's dominion, underscores the truth that the knowledge of God can penetrate and change even the most obstinate of minds.

Rahab: From Harlotry to the Lineage of Christ

Rahab's story is a testament to the impact of faith on a person's life trajectory. A Canaanite harlot, she demonstrated her *emunah* (faith) in Jehovah by hiding Israelite spies (Joshua 2:1-21). Her mind was renewed through the recognition of Jehovah's power and purpose for His people. As a result of her faith, she was not only spared but also grafted into the lineage of Jesus (Matthew 1:5), indicating a complete redefinition of her identity and destiny.

Jonah: From Reluctance to Reluctant Obedience

The prophet Jonah experienced a transformation from reluctance to obedience, though it required a dramatic intervention involving a great fish (Jonah 1:17). His initial flight from Jehovah's commission illustrates the resistance of the human mind to divine purposes. However, after his deliverance and renewed commission, Jonah's *leb* (heart) was realigned to God's will, albeit grudgingly. His mission to Nineveh and its subsequent repentance demonstrate the ripple effect of one individual's transformation.

These biblical examples offer vivid illustrations of the potential for human minds and lives to be transformed through divine intervention and the embrace of God's revelation. They show that the renewal of the mind is not a singular event but a dynamic process that may involve dramatic encounters with God, the gradual revelation of truth, and the daily application of faith. Each story is a compelling narrative of the *dunamis* (power) of God to redirect the course of a life from a trajectory of self-determination to one of divine purpose. These transformations stand as enduring witnesses to the potential for all believers to experience the renewal of their minds and the subsequent metamorphosis of their lives.

Measuring Our Transformation: Growth and Change Over Time

In the grand narrative of Scripture, the concept of transformation is central to the Christian experience. The imperative given by Paul in Romans 12:2, to "be transformed by the renewal of your mind," serves as the theological cornerstone for understanding the gradual and persistent change that is expected to take place within a believer's life. This transformation is not a stagnant occurrence but a continuous process that can be measured over time. It is an *anakainosis* (renewal) that signifies a profound change from one state to another—a metamorphosis in our *nous* (mind) that reflects the dynamic process of sanctification.

The transformation of the *nous* is reflected in various ways throughout one's spiritual journey. It often starts with an initial recognition of one's own sinful nature and the need for redemption. This recognition is not merely intellectual acknowledgment but a deep-seated realization that permeates the heart (*kardia*), impacting the entire being. As Jeremiah stated, the heart is "deceitful above all things and desperately sick" (Jeremiah 17:9), highlighting the necessity for this renewal.

In the *septuagint*, the word *nous* is used to convey the understanding of the mind, the seat of reflective consciousness. It is in this inner space that a battle rages—a battle for truth against the falsehoods that have taken root over a lifetime. As we immerse ourselves in the teachings of the Scriptures, we allow the divine wisdom (*sophia*) to challenge and uproot these deceptions. The transformation is a restructuring of our mental frameworks, where God's truth supersedes former beliefs, and our actions begin to align with His will.

The Incremental Nature of Transformation

The nature of this transformation is incremental. It's a progressive journey marked by small, sometimes imperceptible changes that accumulate over time. Take, for example, the concept of *agape* (love) in the Christian life. Initially, a believer might understand *agape* as a form of affection or benevolence. However, as they grow in their faith, studying passages like 1 Corinthians 13, they begin to appreciate *agape* as the self-sacrificing love demonstrated by Christ—a love that surpasses mere feelings and is made manifest in actions.

Similarly, the fruits of the Spirit—*agape* (love), *chara* (joy), *eirene* (peace), *makrothumia* (patience), *chrestotes* (kindness), *agathosune* (goodness), *pistis* (faithfulness), *prautes* (gentleness), and *egkrateia* (self-control)—are not imparted to believers fully formed. They develop and ripen over time, through continuous interaction with the Word of God and obedience to it.

Transformative Growth Through Trials

The process of transformation is also reflected in how believers respond to trials and suffering. James encourages believers to consider it pure joy when facing trials of various kinds because the testing of faith produces *hypomone* (perseverance) (James 1:2-3). As one matures in faith, the initial despair that might accompany hardships gives way to a steadfastness that understands suffering as a means of growth. This shift in perspective is a clear indication of a renewing mind that begins to view life's challenges through the lens of Scripture rather than through the lens of human understanding.

Behavioral Evidence of Transformation

Behavioral changes are another tangible measure of the mind's renewal. Paul's exhortation to put off the old self and to put on the new self, created after the likeness of God in true righteousness and holiness (Ephesians 4:22-24), signifies a call to action that is observable. A lying tongue becomes committed to truth; where there was once uncontrolled anger, there is now self-control; where greed once dwelt, there is now generosity. These are not mere external modifications but the outworking of internal renewal.

Communal Reflection of Individual Transformation

Moreover, the transformation of the mind is not solely a private endeavor but one that has a communal dimension. The *ekklesia* (church), as the body of Christ, is collectively called to reflect the mind of Christ. This is seen in the way individuals within the community interact with one another—*tapeinophrosune* (humility), *agape* (love), and *eunoia* (goodwill) become the defining traits of the community's life together. As each member's mind is renewed, the entire community grows into the fullness of Christ, edifying itself in love (Ephesians 4:15-16).

The Ultimate Measure: The Mind of Christ

Ultimately, the measure of our transformation is found in how closely our thought patterns align with those of Christ Himself. Paul speaks of having the mind of Christ (1 Corinthians 2:16), a mind that was preoccupied with the will of the Father and characterized by obedience and humility. The journey of transformation, therefore, is one that progressively shapes the believer's mindset to mirror that of Christ—a process that unfolds throughout the entirety of one's life, leading to maturity and completeness in Him.

In this complex yet rewarding journey of transformation, the Christian is invited to a life-long pursuit of aligning the *nous* with the divine revelation found in Scripture. It is not a pursuit undertaken in one's own strength but one that recognizes the sufficiency of Scripture, provided by God, to guide and grow the believer. As the *logos* of God takes root in the individual's life, the evidence of transformation becomes apparent—not just to the individual but to all those they encounter, showcasing the enduring power of God's Word to effect true change in the human heart and mind.

CHAPTER 7 Keeping the Mind Renewed

Daily Disciplines for a Constantly Renewed Mind

In the quest for spiritual growth, the Christian's mind is the battlefield where the fiercest wars are waged. The constant renewal of the mind is pivotal, as articulated in Romans 12:2, where the apostle Paul admonishes believers to avoid conformation to this world but to be transformed by the renewal of the mind. This renewal is not a singular event but a daily discipline, a continual process that must be engaged in with diligence and intentionality.

Engaging with the Word

The cornerstone of keeping the mind renewed is daily engagement with the Word of God. The Hebrew term *dabar*, often translated as "word," carries a broader connotation, representing the very utterances of Jehovah, potent and life-giving. Similarly, the Greek *logos*, signifies not only the written word but also the living Word, Christ Himself. The Scriptures are not merely texts to be read but the living voice of Jehovah to be heard and obeyed. As Hebrews 4:12 asserts, the word of God is living and active, sharper than any two-edged sword. It penetrates to divide soul and spirit, discerning the thoughts and attitudes of the heart. Hence, daily reading, meditation, and application of Scripture are indispensable in renewing the mind. For example, meditating on passages such as Psalm 1, which extols the virtues of delighting in the law of Jehovah, can recalibrate the mind to align with divine wisdom.

Prayer as Dialogue

Prayer is the conduit through which we maintain an open line of communication with the Creator. It is not a monologue but a dialogue, where we speak to Jehovah and also listen. The concept of *teshuva*, a Hebrew word for repentance, involves a returning to Jehovah, which is a critical aspect of prayer. In the New Testament, *proseuche* (prayer) signifies the dependence of the believer on Jehovah. By prayer, we not only express our desires and concerns but also subject our minds to divine scrutiny, as David invited Jehovah to search him and know his heart in Psalm 139:23. Regular, earnest prayer fosters a spiritual sensitivity, sharpening the conscience, and fine-tuning the mind to discern the leading of Jehovah's spirit as revealed through His Word.

Contemplation and Reflection

Contemplation, or *haga* in Hebrew, refers to speaking, uttering, or murmuring, often in the context of meditation. The practice of *nous* (mind) reflection in the New Testament involves deep, reflective thinking on spiritual truths. Contemplative reflection on Scripture, on Jehovah's character, and His works in history is a discipline that keeps the Christian mind focused on the divine. It involves taking specific truths or events—like the Israelites crossing the Red Sea—and pondering the deeper implications of Jehovah's power and faithfulness in one's own life journey.

Community and Fellowship

The Christian life was never meant to be lived in isolation. The *koinonia* (fellowship) with other believers is a means through which the mind is sharpened. As Proverbs 27:17 suggests, "Iron sharpens iron, and one man sharpens another." The discussions, encouragements, and even corrections received within the body of Christ serve as catalysts for mind renewal. Engaging in activities like group Bible study, where believers delve into texts such as the Pauline epistles, offers an opportunity for the collective mind to be challenged and grown.

Worship and Praise

Worship, both personal and corporate, realigns our minds with the truth of who Jehovah is and our position before Him. The Hebrew term *shachah*, and the Greek *proskuneo*, both often translated as "worship," imply a bowing down or prostration before the divine, symbolizing submission and reverence. Incorporating psalms and hymns, such as the doxology found in Jude 1:24-25, into daily routines, enables the believer to maintain a posture of humility and dependence on Jehovah. Music and song have a unique way of bypassing intellectual barriers and engraving truths upon the heart and mind.

Serving and Giving

Active service and giving are practical expressions of a renewed mind. The act of *diakonia* (service) in the New Testament reflects the love of Christ made manifest through the believer. Whether it is serving in a local soup kitchen or providing for the needs of missionaries, service is a tangible way of demonstrating the love of Jehovah and reinforcing the mind's focus on others above self, as Jesus exemplified in His life.

Fasting and Abstinence

Fasting is a biblical discipline that involves voluntary abstinence from food and other pleasures to focus on prayer and spiritual matters. The Hebrew concept of *tzom*, and the Greek *nesteia* (fasting), both reflect this practice. In a world saturated with sensory overload, fasting is a powerful tool for the believer to detach from worldly distractions and sharpen spiritual acuity. Fasting, as demonstrated by Esther before she approached the king (Esther 4:16), can bring about a heightened state of spiritual awareness and mental clarity.

Confronting and Casting Down

Finally, the renewal of the mind necessitates the active confrontation and casting down of ungodly thoughts, imaginations, and every high thing that exalts itself against the knowledge of Jehovah, as instructed in 2 Corinthians 10:5. This involves not just a passive avoidance of evil thoughts but an active demolition of any mental strongholds that oppose the truth of God. When confronted with thoughts that challenge the knowledge of Jehovah, the believer is to take them captive and make them obedient to Christ, ensuring that the mind is a stronghold of truth rather than a bastion of deceit.

The disciplines outlined above form a comprehensive approach to keeping the Christian mind constantly renewed. This is not a casual endeavor but a critical, daily pursuit that demands commitment and perseverance. By adopting these disciplines, believers can fortify their minds against the onslaughts of secular ideology, and maintain a mental posture that is pliable to the Spirit of Jehovah as revealed in His Word.

The Importance of Regular Scripture Study and Prayer

Within the spiritual life of a believer, the practices of Scripture study and prayer are not merely routines but lifelines that connect us to the heart of our faith. The spiritual vitality and mental renewal we crave are nurtured through these disciplines, as they allow us to engage with Jehovah on a profound level.

Scripture Study as a Foundation for Mental Renewal

The Holy Scriptures offer a profound depth of wisdom, and their study is essential for the believer who seeks to renew their mind. The Hebrew term *talmud*, which refers to the study or learning of the Scriptures, points to an intensive and methodical approach. When we delve into the biblical texts, we are not merely scanning words but are engaging with the *dabar* (דָּבָר, word) of Jehovah, a term used to describe the living and active nature of God's communication to His people.

For instance, the Psalms, written in Hebrew poetry, reveal the emotional and spiritual struggles of their authors. They invite the reader to enter into a state of *selah* (סֶלָה), a term likely suggesting pause and reflection, urging the reader to ponder deeply the majesty and faithfulness of Jehovah. As we study, the Psalms resonate with our struggles, offering comfort and perspective.

Similarly, the wisdom literature, like Proverbs, presents *mashal* (מָשָׁל, proverbial wisdom), rich with analogies and practical life principles. These sayings penetrate the mind, offering guidance for daily living. They encourage the believer to view life's situations through the prism of divine wisdom, which is indispensable for maintaining a renewed mind.

In the New Testament, the Greek term *logos* (λόγος, word) in John 1:1 introduces us to Christ as the living Word, embodying the full expression of Jehovah's truth. Through the study of the Gospels, believers encounter the life and teachings of Jesus, the *logos* made flesh. This encounter is not a historical exercise but a transformative experience as the teachings of Christ, from the Sermon on the Mount to His parables, challenge and reshape our thinking.

The Pauline epistles, laden with theological depth, address the mind directly. Phrases such as "be transformed by the renewal of your mind" in Romans 12:2 are not merely doctrinal statements but a call to a radical internal metamorphosis. The Greek term *metanoia* (μετάνοια, change of mind) implies a comprehensive turning around of one's life and perspective. As believers study these epistles, they engage with *sophia* (σοφία, wisdom) and *gnosis* (γνῶσις, knowledge) that undergird the faith, leading to a life more reflective of Christ's nature.

Prayer as the Breath of the Soul

Just as the body requires oxygen to survive, the soul needs prayer for its sustenance. The Hebrew term *tefillah* (תְּפִלָּה, prayer) conveys the sense of intercession, reflection, and self-examination before Jehovah. In the New Testament, *proseuche* (προσευχή, prayer) is often used to indicate the act of bringing our requests and praises before God.

Prayer is more than presenting a list of requests; it is an intimate dialogue. The Psalms again serve as a prime example, often structured as a personal address to Jehovah, expressing the full gamut of human emotion—from anguish to elation. As believers engage in prayer, they align their will with Jehovah's purposes, echoing the *kardia* (καρδία, heart) of Christ, who taught His disciples to pray for Jehovah's will to be done on earth as it is in heaven.

In the act of prayer, believers are reminded of their reliance on Jehovah for wisdom, as James 1:5 encourages the reader to ask God who gives generously to all without reproach. The Greek concept of *sophia* is integral here, referring not just to intellectual knowledge but to practical wisdom for living out one's faith.

When prayer is combined with Scripture study, it becomes a reciprocal exchange where the believer speaks to Jehovah through prayer and listens to Him through His Word. For example, after meditating on a passage from the epistles, a believer might pray for the *dunamis* (δύναμις, power) to apply Paul's teachings on love and unity within their local congregation.

In both Hebrew and Greek, the terms used for prayer convey a sense of urgency and dependency. They denote a conversation that occurs in the inner sanctum of the believer's heart, a *kodesh* (קֹדֶשׁ, holy place) where one stands transparent before Jehovah.

To sustain a renewed mind, it is crucial that these practices are not sporadic but regular. As manna was given daily to Israel during their wilderness journey, so must the believer daily seek the spiritual nourishment of Scripture and prayer. In doing so, they create a *kavanah* (כַּוָּנָה, intention or direction of the heart) that is oriented towards Jehovah, fostering a mind continually refreshed and aligned with the divine will.

This holistic approach ensures that the renewal of the mind is not a one-time event but a continual process. It requires discipline, commitment, and a heart that yearns for the deep things of Jehovah, as the psalmist expressed, "As a deer pants for flowing streams, so pants my soul for you, O God" (Psalm 42:1). By steadfastly engaging in the study of Scripture and the practice of prayer, the believer is equipped to face the battle for the Christian mind with the full armor of God.

Avoiding Complacency: Staying Vigilant in Our Thought Life

In the journey of faith, vigilance is a command, not a suggestion. The apostle Peter warns us to "be sober-minded; be watchful," for the adversary prowls like a roaring lion (1 Peter 5:8). The Greek term *nēphō* (νήφω), translated as "be sober-minded," involves a clarity and control of thought, an alertness that is critical for the believer. This is particularly true for the thought life of a Christian, where complacency can be as dangerous as outright sin. It is a subtle enemy that can cause a gradual but significant drift from the truths of Jehovah.

The danger of a complacent mind is that it can become an incubator for spiritual decay. In the Hebraic understanding, the heart (*leb*, לֵב) is not just the seat of emotions but the center of thought and will. When the heart grows complacent, the individual is no longer standing guard over their thoughts and actions. It is in this unguarded space that seeds of doubt, fear, and disobedience can take root, eventually bearing fruit that is not in keeping with righteousness.

Vigilance Against Satanic Propaganda

The apostle Paul understood the battle that rages for the mind and emphasized the need for spiritual weaponry. He uses the term *logismos* (λογισμός, argument) to describe the high things that set themselves up against the knowledge of God (2 Corinthians 10:5). This indicates that thoughts and reasonings need to be taken captive, suggesting a proactivity in countering false ideologies and philosophies that may subtly influence one's faith.

Satan's propaganda aims to warp the truth of Jehovah's Word, and his tactics are not always overt. Sometimes, it is the slow drip of worldliness, the erosion of conviction through societal norms, or the distortion of Scripture that causes believers to become desensitized. For example, the idea of moral relativism is pervasive in society, and without vigilance, a believer might begin to question the absolute truths of the Scriptures. The Greek concept of *aletheia* (ἀλήθεια, truth) must remain the standard against which all thoughts are measured.

Edward D. Andrews

The Treachery of the Human Heart

Jeremiah warns us of the heart's deceitful nature (*akov*, עָקֹב, deceitful) and its sickness beyond cure (Jeremiah 17:9). Without constant renewal through the Scriptures, the heart can lead one astray. This is why vigilance in our thought life is critical; it involves regularly examining our motivations and desires through the lens of Scripture. The Psalms often reflect this introspective practice, as the psalmist asks Jehovah to search his heart and lead him in the way everlasting (Psalm 139:23-24).

The Callused Conscience

The conscience, which Paul describes as bearing witness in our hearts (Romans 2:15), can either accuse or excuse us. The Greek term *suneidēsis* (συνείδησις, conscience) implies a knowledge within oneself, an internal barometer of right and wrong. However, when ignored, the conscience can become hardened (*porōsis*, πώρωσις), no longer sensitive to the promptings of Scriptural truths. An example of this hardening can be seen in the Pharisees, who, despite their knowledge of the Law, had hearts that were calloused to the essence of Jehovah's commands—justice, mercy, and faithfulness (Matthew 23:23).

Maintaining a Lowliness of Mind

The mind of Christ is characterized by humility or lowliness of mind (*tapeinophrosynē*, ταπεινοφροσύνη). In Philippians 2:5-8, Paul lays out the mindset of Christ, who, though He was in the form of God, did not count equality with God a thing to be grasped. This mindset is antithetical to complacency, for it requires an ongoing attitude of servitude and self-examination. Lowliness of mind is a safeguard against the pride that can inflate the ego and cloud judgment.

Embracing the Mind of Christ

Acquiring the mind of Christ is an active pursuit, one that involves embracing the wisdom and knowledge of Jehovah as revealed through His Word. Paul's exhortation to "have this mind among yourselves, which is yours in Christ Jesus" (Philippians 2:5), underscores the communal aspect of this pursuit. It is in the fellowship of believers that we are reminded of the truths of Scripture and encouraged to maintain a mindset that reflects our Savior.

In understanding *sunetos* (συνετός, intelligent, prudent) as used in 1 Corinthians 2:12-14, it is not merely intellectual assent to doctrinal truths but a deep-seated embrace of these truths, which transforms the believer's way of living. The unbeliever may reject these truths as foolishness (*mōria*, μωρία), but the believer sees them as the very wisdom of God.

The Role of Scripture in Thought Vigilance

The Bible, the Spirit-inspired Word of God, is the believer's manual for mind renewal. It is through the *rhēma* (ῥῆμα, spoken word) of God that we are able to discern truth from error, righteousness from wickedness. When Paul speaks of the "sword of the Spirit, which is the word of God" (Ephesians 6:17), he is referring to the active and living nature of Scripture in combating the forces that seek to corrupt our thoughts.

In conclusion, the battle for the Christian mind is waged daily, and complacency is the enemy that allows the fortresses of sin to be built within our thought life. Vigilance is the steady, constant watch over the heart and mind, discerning every thought and intent through the truth of Jehovah's Word. It is in this disciplined practice that believers are transformed and equipped to stand firm against the schemes of the adversary, ever mindful of the need to "be transformed by the renewal of your mind" (Romans 12:2).

The Community of Believers as a Support System

In the complex fabric of Christian living, the community of believers is indispensable in maintaining a renewed mind. The New Testament Greek term for the community, *ekklesia* (ἐκκλησία), signifies more than a mere assembly; it denotes a body of individuals called out from the world and united in faith. This community is not a peripheral concept to Christian identity but central, for it is within this context that individual transformation is nurtured and safeguarded.

The Function of Fellowship

Fellowship, or *koinonia* (κοινωνία), is the sharing of common life and purpose among believers. It serves as a spiritual ecosystem where members sustain one another, much like the interlocking roots of trees in a forest. The early church, as described in Acts 2:42, devoted themselves to the apostles' teaching, fellowship, the breaking of bread, and prayers. These activities were not just religious formalities but were means by which the mind was continually set upon divine things, fostering a collective consciousness that was saturated with Scriptural principles.

Encouragement and Edification

Within the community, believers are called to encourage (*parakaleō*, παρακαλέω) one another, as seen in Hebrews 3:13, which warns against the hardening of the heart through the deceitfulness of sin. The act of encouragement is not merely offering kind words but involves exhorting and urging each other to remain steadfast in the faith. Similarly, edification, or *oikodomē* (οἰκοδομή), refers to the building up of one another in spiritual maturity and understanding. The apostle Paul speaks of edification as the objective of spiritual gifts (1 Corinthians 14:12), highlighting the importance of using one's God-given abilities for the common good, strengthening the collective mind of the church.

Corrective Community through Accountability

The community also functions as an agent of correction. Galatians 6:1 instructs those who are spiritual to restore someone caught in sin with a spirit of gentleness. The Greek word *katartizō* (καταρτίζω) denotes a restoration to proper condition. It is through loving and truthful confrontation that the community helps guard the mind against deception and moral drift. This is not merely about righting wrongs but about realigning the believer's thoughts and attitudes with the truth of the Scriptures.

The Power of Corporate Worship

Corporate worship plays a significant role in renewing the mind. When believers sing psalms, hymns, and spiritual songs together, as advised in Colossians 3:16, they are not only expressing praise but also reinforcing Scriptural truths in their hearts and minds. The shared experience of worship, with its focus on Jehovah's attributes and acts, serves as a repeated recalibration of our perceptions and priorities.

Teaching and Discipleship

In the community of believers, the role of sound teaching and discipleship is paramount. The Greek word *didaskalia* (διδασκαλία), which means teaching, is a foundational component for a renewed mind. As Paul advised Timothy, the public reading of Scripture, preaching, and teaching (1 Timothy 4:13) are essential for maintaining doctrinal purity and practical application of the Word. Discipleship involves a relational process where mature believers, through life-on-life interaction, instill wisdom (*sophia*, σοφία) and understanding (*sunesis*, σύνεσις) in less mature believers, guiding them in their spiritual growth.

Confession and Prayer

James 5:16 emphasizes the importance of confessing sins to one another and praying for one another for healing. The confession is more than an admission of guilt; it is a deliberate exposure of one's struggles and weaknesses to the light of community accountability. Prayer, in this context, is not a solitary act but a corporate weapon wielded together in spiritual warfare. Through prayer, believers collectively harness the power (*dunamis*, δύναμις) of God for personal and communal transformation.

The Sharing of Burdens

The community of believers is also a place for sharing burdens. Galatians 6:2 instructs believers to bear one another's burdens, thus fulfilling the law of Christ. The word for burden, *baros* (βάρος), suggests a weight or heaviness that is too much for one person to carry alone. It is within the context of the community that the psychological and spiritual burdens are distributed, making them more bearable and demonstrating the practical outworking of love.

Modeling Christlike Humility

A vital characteristic that the community fosters is the lowliness of mind which Jesus exemplified. In Philippians 2:3-5, believers are exhorted to do nothing from selfish ambition but to regard others as more significant than themselves, following the mind of Christ, who, though He was in the form of God, humbled Himself. This mindset is counter-cultural and counter-intuitive to the natural human inclination towards pride and self-promotion. The community serves as a training ground for cultivating this humility, as believers learn to serve and esteem others above themselves.

Resistance Against Satanic Propaganda

In a world where satanic propaganda and ideologies seek to mold the believer's mind, the community stands as a bulwark of resistance. It embodies the collective strength described in Ecclesiastes 4:12, where a threefold cord is not quickly broken. Through unity in the truth and mutual support, the community helps its members to resist the lies that so often besiege the mind, affirming the transformative power of the gospel.

In every respect, the community of believers is integral to the process of mind renewal. It is in this divinely instituted matrix that Christians find the resources for mutual care, growth, and the continual realignment of their thinking with the will of Jehovah, as expressed in His inspired Word. The renewed mind is thus a corporate pursuit, achieved not in isolation but in the dynamic interplay of relationships, worship, teaching, and joint striving for the faith of the gospel.

CHAPTER 8 Spiritual Sicknesses of Mind and Heart

Diagnosing Spiritual Sickness: Symptoms and Causes

Spiritual sickness, often less tangible than physical illness, can be equally devastating to the Christian mind and heart. It disrupts the believer's harmony with Jehovah and His divine statutes, resulting in symptoms and causes that are crucial to recognize and understand.

Symptoms of Spiritual Sickness

The Scriptures lay bare the symptoms of a spiritually sick heart. In Proverbs 4:23, Solomon admonishes to "keep your heart with all vigilance, for from it flow the springs of life." The Hebrew word *leb* (לֵב), translated as "heart," refers not merely to emotions but to the seat of thoughts, will, and moral actions. When spiritual sickness invades the *leb*, it can manifest in various forms:

- **Doubt and Unbelief**: Like a noxious weed in a garden, doubt can choke the flourishing faith of a believer. The Greek term *apistia* (ἀπιστία), or unbelief, reflects a state of mind that is not convinced of Jehovah's truth or faithfulness. This symptom can stem from neglecting the Word of God, leading to a forgetfulness of His promises and character.

- **Fear and Anxiety**: Chronic worry is another symptom of spiritual malaise. The word *merimna* (μεριμνα) in Philippians 4:6 conveys a divided or distracted mind overly concerned with the cares of this life. It reveals a heart that is struggling to rest in Jehovah's sovereignty and care.

- **Despondency and Loss of Hope**: A disquieted and despondent spirit, described as a "broken spirit" in Proverbs

17:22, *ruach nishbarah* (רוּחַ נְשָׁבָרָה), can dry up the bones and deplete the vitality of one's inner life. When hope is deferred or lost, the heart becomes sick.

- **Moral Compromise**: When sin is rationalized rather than repented of, it signals a severe ailment in the believer's life. *Anomia* (ἀνομία), lawlessness or iniquity, as mentioned in 1 John 3:4, indicates a mind that has deviated from the righteous standards of God's Word.

- **Spiritual Lethargy**: A lukewarm state, neither hot nor cold as described in Revelation 3:16, shows a spiritual lethargy that disgusts Jehovah. This apathy toward spiritual matters is a dangerous symptom of a heart that has lost its first love for God and His truth.

Causes of Spiritual Sickness

Identifying the causes behind these symptoms is critical to the healing process. Several factors can lead to spiritual sickness:

- **Neglect of Scripture**: Just as the body withers without nourishment, the mind becomes feeble without the sustenance of God's Word. The Greek term *logos* (λόγος), referring to the Word, is described as living and active in Hebrews 4:12. When neglected, the mind lacks the discernment necessary to navigate life's complexities.

- **Worldly Influences**: The system of things, *kosmos* (κόσμος) in the Greek, can seep into the believer's consciousness, leading to a gradual acceptance of ungodly values and behaviors. 1 John 2:15-16 warns against the love of the world and its desires that are at enmity with Jehovah.

- **Unconfessed Sin**: Sin, when hidden or unacknowledged, creates a barrier between the believer and Jehovah. The Psalmist expresses in Psalm 32:3 that when he kept silent about his sin, his bones wasted away. The Hebrew *chata* (חָטָא), to miss the mark, signifies the deviation from God's standard that, when unconfessed, festers in the soul.

- **Isolation from Fellowship**: A believer isolated from the community of faith, *koinonia* (κοινωνία), deprives themselves of the mutual support and accountability that is vital for spiritual health. Hebrews 10:25 urges not to forsake assembling together, as is the habit of some, but to encourage one another.

- **Persistent Trials and Sufferings**: While trials can produce endurance, relentless sufferings without spiritual support or understanding can wear down the heart. The Greek word *peirasmos* (πειρασμός) in James 1:2 refers to trials of various kinds that, without a proper focus on Jehovah's purposes, can lead to discouragement.

- **Satanic Assaults**: The adversary, *diabolos* (διάβολος), is ever-seeking to devour. Ephesians 6:11 talks about the schemes of the devil, which aim to corrupt the mind with lies and accusations. These spiritual attacks can lead to doubts and confusion if the believer is not grounded in the truth.

In conclusion, spiritual sickness is a debilitating condition that affects both mind and heart, observable through a range of symptoms stemming from various causes. A thorough diagnosis of these spiritual ailments involves a critical and honest self-examination in the light of Scripture. It requires believers to recognize the severity of their condition and to seek the remedy in Jehovah's Word, in fellowship with other believers, in confession and repentance, and in a relentless fight against the influence of sin, the world, and Satan. Only then can a believer truly experience the transformative power of the Holy Spirit working through the Word, renewing the mind, and restoring the heart to spiritual health and vitality.

The Dangers of Letting Spiritual Illness Go Untreated

In the labyrinth of the Christian life, the mind and heart operate as the compass and engine, directing and driving the believer's thoughts, actions, and spiritual vitality. When these integral parts suffer from spiritual sickness, it is as if the compass is skewed and the engine sputters, leading to a journey fraught with confusion and stagnation.

Just as a physical ailment can worsen if left unchecked, a spiritual illness of the mind and heart, when neglected, can have dire consequences.

The Erosion of Discernment

The *nous* (νοῦς), or mind, is where discernment is honed, acting as the adjudicator of truth and error. Spiritual sickness skews the believer's spiritual perception, clouding the mind's eye that should see clearly the distinction between holy and profane, true and false. This erosion of discernment is like a ship's captain losing the ability to navigate in a storm, where even the North Star is obscured by thick clouds of falsehood.

Faltering Faith and Weakening Conviction

Faith, *pistis* (πίστις), and conviction are the sinews and bones of the Christian life. When spiritual maladies infiltrate the *kardia* (καρδιά), the heart, faith can begin to atrophy, and conviction may wane like a muscle unexercised. The once firm stance in Jehovah's promises and commands becomes a tottering gait, susceptible to every wind of doctrine that blows with persuasive eloquence or cultural appeal.

Hardening of the Heart

The Scriptures speak of the heart that can become hard as stone, resistant to Jehovah's molding. The *porosis* (πώρωσις) of the heart, a hardening or callousness, makes it impervious to the convicting power of God's Word. It is the spiritual equivalent of a medical condition where the arteries are clogged, preventing the life-giving flow of blood; here, it is the spirit's responsiveness that is stifled.

Spiritual Isolation

An untreated spiritual illness often leads to self-imposed isolation. The neglect of the means by which Jehovah fortifies the believer, including fellowship with other believers, study of Scripture, and prayer, can be compared to a soldier abandoning their post. This isolation becomes a fertile ground for the *diabolos* (διάβολος), the devil, to sow seeds of doubt and despair, as there is strength in the community, *koinonia* (κοινωνία), which is sapped in solitude.

Vulnerability to False Teachings

The spiritual sickness of mind and heart leaves a believer vulnerable to false teachings. A weakened state of spiritual health is like a compromised immune system; just as the body may fail to recognize and combat pathogens, the spiritually sick may fail to discern and reject false doctrines. The result is a susceptibility to be "tossed back and forth by the waves, and blown here and there by every wind of teaching" (Ephesians 4:14).

Loss of Witness and Influence

A Christian is called to be a light to the world, a beacon of truth and hope. However, spiritual sickness dims this light, muddying the clarity of witness that should shine forth. The believer's influence, both within the Christian community and in the broader world, is significantly compromised, mirroring a city on a hill whose lights have been extinguished.

Disrupted Relationship with Jehovah

Perhaps the most tragic consequence of untreated spiritual illness is the disruption it causes in the relationship with Jehovah. Just as Adam and Eve hid in shame, the spiritually ill often retreat from the presence of God, avoiding the light of His holiness that exposes sin and calls for repentance. The *anomia* (ἀνομία), lawlessness, that results from this separation marks a life that has strayed from the path of righteousness.

Internal Turmoil and Loss of Peace

The inner peace that surpasses understanding, *eirene* (εἰρήνη), is a casualty of spiritual sickness. The turmoil that churns within can be likened to the tumultuous waves of a storm-tossed sea. Where there once was the tranquility of a steadfast spirit, there now exists an internal chaos that robs the believer of the serene assurance that Jehovah governs in the affairs of men and their hearts.

Eternal Consequences

While all consequences of spiritual sickness are severe, the most sobering are the eternal ramifications. If left untreated, the gradual drift from Jehovah's ways can become a permanent state, leading to a forfeiture of the promises and joys of everlasting life. The *telos* (τέλος), the end, of such neglect is not merely temporal discomfort but an eternal separation from the source of life itself.

In the face of these severe dangers, the prescription for the believer is clear and urgent: to be vigilant in self-examination, steadfast in prayer, diligent in studying the Scriptures, and quick to embrace the fellowship of believers. Only by such means can the Christian mind and heart be fortified against the pernicious effects of spiritual sickness and be transformed by the renewal of the mind, as instructed in Romans 12:2.

Prescriptions for Healing: Biblical Counsel and Christian Fellowship

In confronting the pervasive maladies of the mind and heart that afflict believers, Scripture provides *prescriptions* that are as potent and transformative today as they were two millennia ago. Within the pages of God's Word, we find the *therapeia* (θεραπεία), or healing, for the spiritual sicknesses that undermine the *nous* (νοῦς, mind) and *kardia* (καρδιά, heart), urging a return to wholeness through Christ. Healing from these ailments requires an immersion into biblical truths and a deliberate engagement with the community of believers, the body of Christ.

The Primacy of Scripture in Spiritual Healing

The *logos* (λόγος, Word) of God stands as the ultimate *iatreion* (ἰατρεῖον, hospital) for the soul. It is within the sacred text that the mind is renewed and realigned with divine truth. In the struggle against spiritual sickness, Hebrews 4:12 asserts the Word of God is living and active, sharper than any double-edged sword, discerning thoughts and intentions of the heart. The Apostle Paul understood the imperative of anchoring one's thoughts to the truth, as he exhorted in Philippians 4:8 to dwell on whatever is true, noble, right, pure, lovely, admirable, excellent, or praiseworthy.

Counsel Rooted in the Historical-Grammatical Interpretation

The historical-grammatical method of interpretation insists on understanding Scripture in its original context, considering the grammar and historical circumstances of the text. The Apostle Paul's letters, including the often-debated Hebrews, are ripe with counsel for correcting the skewed perspective that contributes to spiritual sickness. The counsel found in these texts should not be a balm applied superficially but must penetrate deeply, correcting and guiding the believer toward *orthopraxy*, right conduct, that stems from *orthodoxy*, right belief.

Christian Fellowship as a Catalyst for Healing

The *koinonia* (κοινωνία, fellowship) of believers serves as a crucible for the refinement of the believer's character. Just as iron sharpens iron, so one person sharpens another (Proverbs 27:17). The early church in Acts devoted themselves to the apostles' teaching and to fellowship, to the breaking of bread and to prayer (Acts 2:42). It is in the context of fellowship that the *allelon* (ἀλλήλων, one another) commands of the New Testament find their fullest expression: Encourage one another, bear one another's burdens, confess your sins to one another. This mutual edification is a safeguard against the deceitfulness of sin that can harden the heart.

The Role of Biblical Counsel in the Local Church

Within the local church, *presbuteros* (πρεσβύτερος, elders) and teachers are tasked with providing counsel that is anchored in

Scripture. Through teaching, reproof, correction, and training in righteousness (2 Timothy 3:16), these leaders serve to guide the congregation in the path of spiritual health. Biblical counsel is not a mere transfer of information but an intimate impartation of wisdom that calls for a response, an *epistrophē* (ἐπιστροφή, turning) to God.

Confession and Repentance: The Path to Restoration

Confession and repentance are essential in the journey toward healing. The *exomologesis* (ἐξομολόγησις, confession) of sin and the *metanoia* (μετάνοια, repentance) that follows is not just a change of mind but a transformation of the heart and life direction. The Psalms offer numerous examples, such as David's contrite spirit in Psalm 51, where he acknowledges his transgressions and seeks restoration with Jehovah.

The Proactive Discipline of the Mind

To combat the onslaught of negative and impure thoughts, the believer must exercise the *dunamis* (δύναμις, power) provided by God through His Word to take every thought captive and make it obedient to Christ (2 Corinthians 10:5). This involves a proactive discipline, a *gumnasia* (γυμνασία, exercise) of the mind, wherein every thought is evaluated and subjected to the truth of Scripture.

Living Out the Renewed Mind in Community

The renewed mind must find expression in the life of the community. Paul's exhortation in Romans 12:2 to be transformed by the renewal of the mind is followed by an imperative to live out this renewed mind in the body of Christ, serving one another with the gifts given by God. The 'mind of Christ' is not merely a private spiritual plateau but is demonstrated in love, service, and unity within the Christian fellowship.

The Place of Prayer in Spiritual Wholeness

Prayer is the *pneuma* (πνεῦμα, breath) of the Christian life, a vital aspect of both personal devotion and community life. In Philippians 4:6-7, Paul urges believers to bring everything to God in prayer, and the peace of God, which transcends all understanding, will guard their hearts and minds in Christ Jesus. Through prayer, believers are aligned with God's will, and their requests become the expressions of a heart in tune with divine purposes.

Encouragement from Pastoral Examples

The Scriptures provide *paradeigmata* (παραδείγματα, examples) of those who have fought the good fight of faith. Timothy is instructed to set an example in speech, in conduct, in love, in faith, in purity (1 Timothy 4:12). The *episkopoi* (ἐπίσκοποι, overseers) and *diakonoi* (διάκονοι, deacons) of the church are to be models of virtue, providing a living *hypogrammos* (ὑπογραμμός, pattern) for the flock to follow.

Avoidance of Spiritual Contamination

The believer must be wary of false teachings that can infiltrate and corrupt the mind. The counsel of 1 John 4:1 to test the spirits to see whether they are from God is a necessary precaution in a world where false prophets have gone out into the world. The wisdom from above, as described in James 3:17, is pure, peace-loving, considerate, submissive, full of mercy and good fruit, impartial, and sincere—a stark contrast to the wisdom of the world.

In sum, the biblical prescriptions for spiritual sicknesses of the mind and heart are multifaceted, encompassing the study and application of Scripture, engagement in the life and ministry of the church, the practice of confession and repentance, and the cultivation of a prayerful life. These practices work in concert to foster spiritual health, ensuring that the believer is equipped to discern and overcome the wiles of the adversary, drawing ever closer to the image of Christ.

Edward D. Andrews

Recovery and Restoration: Testimonies of Renewed Minds

The *nous* (νοῦς, mind) is the epicenter of spiritual battles; it is where the conflict between God's will and human imperfection rages fiercest. Within this context, the transformative power of God's Word becomes most evident when believers transition from a state of spiritual sickness to wholeness, mirroring the renewing of the mind that the Apostle Paul speaks of in Romans 12:2. This chapter examines the narratives of individuals who have experienced this profound change, casting a light on the potency of Scripture in revolutionizing the human *nous* and *kardia* (καρδιά, heart).

The Prodigal Mind Returned

Consider the parable of the prodigal son (Luke 15:11-32), a story that illustrates the restoration of a life through repentance and forgiveness. The *metanoia* (μετάνοια, repentance) exhibited by the younger son represents a paradigmatic shift from self-reliance to a humble seeking of grace. This narrative unfolds the beauty of recovery as the father embraces the repentant son, symbolizing Jehovah's readiness to receive those who return to Him with a renewed *nous*.

Transformative Encounters with Christ

In the Gospels, we encounter individuals like Zacchaeus (Luke 19:1-10), whose *sunesis* (σύνεσις, understanding) of his condition leads to a radical change. Upon meeting Jesus, Zacchaeus undergoes a heart transformation that propels him from a life of extortion to restitution and generosity. It's a testament to the immediate and far-reaching impact that an encounter with the *logos* made flesh can instill in one's life.

Pauline Paradigms of Renewal

The Apostle Paul himself is a testament to the transformative power of Christ. From a persecutor of Christians to an apostle, his transformation was both radical and complete. His letters offer insight into the renewal of the mind, emphasizing the need for a *kainos* (καινὸς, new) way of thinking as seen in Ephesians 4:22-24, where he encourages the putting off of the old self and being renewed in the spirit of one's mind.

Peter's Path of Recovery

Simon Peter's denial of Christ and subsequent restoration (John 18:15-27; 21:15-19) also serves as a powerful narrative of recovery. Peter's spiritual sickness of fear and denial was met with a restorative conversation with the risen Christ, highlighting the mercy and restorative power of Jehovah that can transform even the most despairing moments into ones of hope and mission.

The Mind Made Whole in Community

The early church, as described in the book of Acts, provides a model for the collective renewal of the mind. The believers' dedication to the apostles' teaching, fellowship, breaking of bread, and prayer (Acts 2:42) exemplifies a community-wide transformation that fortified them against the spiritual maladies of their time. The communal aspect of *koinonia* (κοινωνία, fellowship) cannot be overstated in its role in individual and corporate renewal.

David's Penitential Poetry

In the Hebrew scriptures, the psalms of David offer profound insights into the process of recovery and restoration. Psalms like Psalm 51 convey the depth of David's remorse and his desire for cleansing and renewal before Jehovah. The vivid imagery of being cleansed with hyssop and washed whiter than snow (Psalm 51:7) paints a picture of the mind and heart made clean through Jehovah's forgiveness.

The Prophets on Renewal

The prophetic books contain calls to *shuv* (שׁוּב, return), like the one in Hosea 14:1-2, where Israel is called to return to Jehovah for healing and restoration. The prophets' vivid portrayals of Israel's spiritual sickness coupled with Jehovah's readiness to heal illustrate the divine pattern of initiating recovery and offering restoration to a penitent people.

Wisdom Literature on the Renewed Mind

The wisdom literature, particularly Proverbs, gives practical advice on maintaining a sound mind and heart. It teaches that the fear of Jehovah is the beginning of knowledge (Proverbs 1:7), and wisdom, when internalized, acts as a safeguard against spiritual sickness, as it directs one's paths and decisions.

Contemporary Witnesses

In the present age, there are countless narratives of individuals whose lives have been transformed by the renewing of their minds through Scripture. These stories often start with a realization of spiritual bankruptcy and lead to a quest for truth, culminating in a surrender to the will of Jehovah, manifested in a lifestyle that reflects the mind of Christ.

Each of these stories underscores the reality that spiritual sickness of the mind and heart is not terminal; it can be remedied through the efficacious working of God's Word and Spirit. Jehovah is the *roteh* (רופא, healer) who provides the means for this recovery, and His Word is the medicine that renews and transforms. The consistent element in these testimonies is the movement from a position of spiritual malaise to one of health, illustrating the biblical principle that though the heart is *akrataleēs* (ἀκρατής, without strength), it can be made strong through the *dunamis* (δύναμις, power) of God's transforming grace. These examples serve as *beacons* of hope, affirming the possibility of a renewed mind for those entrapped in spiritual sickness, and they bear witness to the enduring truth that "where the Spirit of the Lord is, there is freedom" (2 Corinthians 3:17).

CHAPTER 9 Dealing with Destructive Self-Defeating Thoughts

Identifying Harmful Thought Patterns and Their Triggers

In the quest for mental and spiritual health, recognizing and understanding destructive self-defeating thoughts is paramount. Such thoughts are often deeply ingrained, stemming from the *yetser* (יצר, inclination) that is skewed towards evil as delineated in Genesis 6:5 and 8:21. This bent of the human heart towards sin is also highlighted by the prophet Jeremiah, who describes the heart as *akob* (עָקֹב, deceitful) and *anash* (אָנֻשׁ, desperate) in Jeremiah 17:9. These inner thought patterns are not only detrimental to our well-being but stand contrary to the divine mandate for believers to have the *nous* (νοῦς, mind) of Christ (1 Corinthians 2:16).

The Apostle Paul was acutely aware of the spiritual warfare waged in the *noemata* (νοήματα, minds) of believers, recognizing that the battlefield is not of flesh but of the spirit (2 Corinthians 10:4). This warfare includes the task of demolishing *ochuromata* (ὀχυρώματα, strongholds) that represent these harmful thought patterns. These strongholds can take many forms, such as persistent doubts about one's worth, habitual pessimism, or a propensity to harbor resentment.

Destructive thought patterns often arise from various triggers. These triggers can be external, such as stressful environments or negative social interactions, or internal, stemming from memories, unmet expectations, or ingrained false beliefs. The recognition of these triggers is crucial for the transformation of the mind (Romans 12:2) because only through identifying them can one begin the process of renewal.

107

The Role of Satanic Influence

The mind is the arena where the adversary, Satan, sows seeds of destruction. He utilizes *diaballo* (διαβάλλω, to slander) and *pseudos* (ψεῦδος, lies) to infect the believer's thought life. Understanding the *methodeia* (μεθοδεία, schemes) of the devil is vital in combatting these thoughts (Ephesians 6:11). It is his wiles that often underpin the triggers of harmful thoughts, exploiting our weaknesses and past experiences.

Unpacking the Layers of Harmful Thoughts

To address these issues at their core, one must examine the layers of thought processes. For example, a thought such as "I am unworthy of love" may be a surface reflection of a deeper belief that one's value is contingent upon others' approval. This could stem from a *paidion* (παιδίον, childlike) experience where love was conditional, thus forming a *skolops* (σκόλοψ, thorn) in the mind that festers into adulthood.

Another example might be the recurring thought "I must be perfect," which can lead to excessive self-criticism and fear of failure. This pattern might have been shaped by a *merimna* (μέριμνα, care) to live up to unrealistic standards, whether self-imposed or from external sources, such as parents or societal pressures.

The Trigger of Comparison

The *syneidesis* (συνείδησις, conscience) plays a role in recognizing these destructive patterns. A common trigger is the habit of comparison, which the Scripture advises against (2 Corinthians 10:12). When the mind engages in comparing one's achievements, appearance, or life circumstances to others, it can quickly spiral into jealousy, discontent, or pride.

Facing Past Traumas

Often, the triggers lie dormant within past traumas. An individual may experience a flashback or *mimnesko* (μιμνῄσκω, remember) of a past event, which then evokes the same unhealthy thought patterns experienced during the original event. Addressing these past wounds is a step towards renewing the mind, as it uncovers the root of the thoughts that may now be automatic.

The Influence of Culture and Media

In contemporary society, media and culture exert a powerful influence on thought patterns. The cultural *ethos* (ἦθος, character) often promotes values and norms that are in opposition to biblical teaching, influencing believers to adopt a *phronema* (φρόνημα, mindset) that is antithetical to the mind of Christ.

Practical Steps in Identifying Triggers

To combat these patterns, one must become an observer of one's own thoughts, practicing *nepsis* (νῆψις, watchfulness) as counseled by 1 Peter 5:8. This includes noting the circumstances and emotions that precede negative thought patterns. Keeping a journal can be helpful in tracking these occurrences and examining them in the light of Scripture.

In conclusion, identifying harmful thought patterns and their triggers is a foundational step in the battle for the Christian mind. It requires vigilance, self-awareness, and a commitment to apply the truths of Scripture. As one engages in this process, the *anakainosis* (ἀνακαίνωσις, renewal) of the mind becomes a tangible reality, leading to a life that more fully reflects the transformative power of the Word of God.

Edward D. Andrews

Combating Negative Thoughts with Biblical Truth

In the battlefield of the mind, the persistent siege of negative thoughts can be debilitating. To fortify the mind, it is essential to grasp firmly the hilt of Scripture, wielding it not only as a defensive bulwark but also as a proactive weapon to dispel the shadows cast by such thoughts. This spiritual strategy is rooted in the understanding that every thought must be made captive to obey Christ (2 Corinthians 10:5).

The Authority of Scripture

Central to combating negative thoughts is the recognition of the authority of Scripture (*graphe* γραφή). The Bible is not merely a collection of historical accounts and moral guidelines but the inspired Word of God (*theopneustos* θεόπνευστος), profitable for teaching, for reproof, for correction, and for training in righteousness (2 Timothy 3:16). It serves as the ultimate source of truth, against which all thoughts, beliefs, and philosophies must be measured.

Discerning the Nature of Thoughts

To differentiate between destructive thoughts and those aligned with biblical truth, one must discern the nature of these thoughts. The term *diakrisis* (διάκρισις), often translated as "discernment," implies a process of thorough examination and judgment. This discernment is honed by engaging with Scripture, allowing the living and active Word (*logos* λόγος) to penetrate and judge the thoughts and intentions of the heart (Hebrews 4:12).

The Process of Renewal

The renewal of the mind is not a passive event but an active, ongoing process. The Apostle Paul's use of the word *anakainosis* (ἀνακαίνωσις) in Romans 12:2 implies a continual renewal, a metamorphosis that occurs as the believer immerses themselves in the

110

truths of Scripture. This transformation is rooted in the rejection of conformity to this age and a robust embrace of the good, acceptable, and perfect will of God.

Example: Combating Fear with God's Sovereignty

For instance, a common self-defeating thought is fear—fear of the future, fear of failure, or fear of man. To combat this, one would reflect on the biblical concept of God's sovereignty (*kuriotēs* κυριότης). Proverbs 19:21 reminds us that many are the plans in a person's heart, but it is the Lord's purpose (*etsah* עֵצָה) that prevails. Meditating on this truth instills the conviction that despite uncertainties, there is a divine orchestration at play.

The Antidote to Doubt: Divine Faithfulness

Doubt is another invasive thought that erodes confidence. Doubt about one's salvation, doubt in God's promises, or doubt in His presence during trials. Scripture offers an antidote in the form of divine faithfulness (*emunah* אֱמוּנָה). Lamentations 3:22-23 assures that the steadfast love of Jehovah never ceases; his mercies never come to an end; they are new every morning; great is your faithfulness. The believer is called to remember and recount the Lord's faithfulness as a means to dispel doubt.

Rejecting Lies with the Belt of Truth

Lies about self-worth, lies about one's purpose, and lies that fuel condemnation must be countered with the belt of truth (*alētheia* ἀλήθεια), as described in the full armor of God (Ephesians 6:14). Truth fortifies the believer, offering a secure foundation. For instance, when thoughts of worthlessness arise, one is to remember that they are God's workmanship (*poiēma* ποίημα), created in Christ Jesus for good works (Ephesians 2:10).

Edward D. Andrews

The Assurance of God's Promises

Holding on to the assurance of God's promises combats the hopelessness that often infiltrates the mind. Abraham, for example, was commended for not wavering through unbelief regarding the promise of God but was strengthened in his faith and gave glory to God, fully persuaded that God had the power to do what he had promised (Romans 4:20-21). The believer, therefore, is to imitate such faith, clinging to the *epaggelia* (ἐπαγγελία, promises) of God as an anchor for the soul.

The Refutation of Condemnation

Condemnation is a frequent invader of the mind, suggesting that one is not truly forgiven or that past sins define the present. In response, Romans 8:1 asserts there is now no condemnation for those who are in Christ Jesus. The word *katakrima* (κατάκριμα) denotes a penalty or punishment from which believers are set free. The realization of this liberation is vital in rejecting the falsehood of enduring condemnation.

Encouragement Through Community

Isolation can amplify negative thoughts, whereas community—fellowship with other believers—provides a platform for encouragement and accountability. As Proverbs 27:17 states, iron sharpens iron, and one man sharpens another (*barzel* בַּרְזֶל). This communal aspect of faith is crucial for the individual's growth and fortification against the assault of destructive thoughts.

Visualizing Victory through Prayer

Visualizing spiritual victory plays a pivotal role in overcoming negative thoughts. Prayer (*proseuchē* προσευχή) is the means by which believers lay their burdens before Jehovah and visualize the outcome rooted in divine intervention. Philippians 4:6-7 encourages believers not to be anxious about anything, but in every situation, by prayer and petition, with thanksgiving, present your requests to God. The peace of God, which transcends all understanding, will guard your hearts and your minds in Christ Jesus.

In summation, combating negative thoughts with biblical truth is a deliberate act of faith, requiring the believer to engage with the entirety of Scripture, apply its principles to every thought, and live in the assured hope that comes from the promises of God. By this approach, the Christian mind is guarded, guided, and ultimately transformed.

Strategies for Replacing Destructive Thoughts with Constructive Ones

In the arena of the mind, believers are called to engage in a continuous process of casting down destructive self-defeating thoughts and replacing them with constructive, life-giving truths. This process is rooted in the understanding that the thoughts we entertain shape our beliefs and, consequently, our actions. Thus, the believer must adopt a proactive stance, equipping themselves with the transformative power of God's Word.

Engaging with the Authority of Scripture

The authoritative standard for all thoughts is the inspired Scripture, which possesses the divine *dunamis* (δύναμις, power) to demolish strongholds of faulty thinking. To engage effectively with Scripture, one must acknowledge its inerrant nature, allowing it to permeate every aspect of their cognitive realm. This engagement involves both a heartfelt meditation on God's promises and a rigorous application of these truths to everyday thought patterns.

Identifying the Root of Negative Thoughts

One must first identify the *akar* (עָקָר, root) of destructive thoughts. Whether stemming from past experiences, personal failures, or external influences, these thoughts often find fertile ground in a heart not fortified by truth. Identifying these roots requires honest self-examination under the light of Scriptural teaching.

The Role of Confession and Repentance

The first step in replacing destructive thoughts is the acknowledgment of their presence, followed by confession and repentance. The *metanoia* (μετάνοια, repentance) that Scripture speaks of involves a complete change of mind, a turning away from negative patterns and a turning toward God. It is about recognizing the disparity between one's thoughts and the mind of Christ and seeking to align the two.

Harnessing the Power of Divine Promises

Once identified, the believer can begin to actively refute negative thoughts with the promises of God. For example, thoughts of inadequacy can be replaced by meditating on Philippians 4:13, which states, "I can do all things through him who strengthens me." The term *ischuo* (ἰσχύω, to be strong) here implies a strength that comes not from within but from Christ Himself.

Visualizing Spiritual Truths

Creating mental images of biblical truths can be a powerful strategy. Visualizing oneself wearing the full armor of God, as described in Ephesians 6, can reinforce the truth that one is fully equipped to stand against the schemes of the devil. This visual strategy helps to internalize the reality that the believer is not defenseless but empowered by God Himself.

Transformative Prayer

Engaging in transformative prayer—bringing every destructive thought before God—enables believers to actively depend on His power. This type of prayer is not passive but rather a *krauge* (κραυγή, earnest pleading) to God for deliverance and strength. It is rooted in the belief that prayer changes things, beginning with the mind of the one who prays.

The Practice of Biblical Affirmation

Biblical affirmation involves speaking truth over oneself. For instance, when the mind whispers that one is unloved, the believer can affirm Romans 8:38-39, which assures that nothing can separate us from the love of God. The term *peitho* (πείθω, to be persuaded) used in this passage signifies a fully convinced state of mind that stands firm against contrary emotions or thoughts.

Cultivating the Fruit of the Spirit

As one grows in the understanding and application of Scripture, the fruit of the Spirit as mentioned in Galatians 5:22-23 should start to replace negative characteristics. Thoughts of anger, bitterness, and envy weaken as love, joy, peace, patience, kindness, goodness, faithfulness, gentleness, and self-control take root and grow. The *karpos* (καρπός, fruit) of the Spirit then becomes the natural byproduct of a mind renewed by truth.

The Practice of Thankfulness

A heart of thankfulness can shift the focus from what is lacking to what has been provided. The practice of *eucharistia* (εὐχαριστία, thanksgiving) can transform one's perspective, redirecting thoughts from negative contemplation to the acknowledgment of God's goodness. As one reflects on God's blessings and character, there is less room for destructive thoughts.

Renewing the Mind Daily

The *anakainosis* (ἀνακαίνωσις, renewal) of the mind is a daily endeavor. Just as manna was gathered fresh each day in the wilderness, so must the believer daily feed on the truths of Scripture. This daily renewal is a proactive stance against the stagnation of the mind, ensuring that it is continually refreshed and aligned with the Word of God.

Fostering a Mind Unified with Believers

Unity with fellow believers offers a buffer against the insidious nature of negative thinking. As members of one body, Christians are called to bear one another's burdens and to speak truth into each other's lives. This unified front stands as a bastion against the enemy's attempts to isolate and overpower the individual mind.

Embracing a Lowliness of Mind

The lowliness of mind (*tapeinophrosyne* ταπεινοφροσύνη, humility) that Christ exemplified is a powerful antidote to thoughts of pride and self-deprecation alike. This humility does not mean self-belittlement but rather the recognition of one's rightful place before God. A mind steeped in humility is resilient against many forms of negative thinking, recognizing both its own weakness and the supreme sufficiency of God.

In conclusion, the strategies for replacing destructive thoughts with constructive ones are multifaceted, involving a holistic approach that encompasses the acknowledgment of the issue, confession, the application of Scripture, prayer, visualization, thankfulness, daily renewal, communal support, and humility. Through these means, believers are equipped to win the battle for their minds, not by their might, but by the power of the Spirit working through the living and active Word of God.

Maintaining Mental Fortitude Through Life's Trials

In the journey of faith, trials are a constant. As believers strive to align their thoughts with the Word of God, they inevitably encounter various trials that challenge their mental fortitude. These challenges range from daily stresses to profound losses and can significantly impact one's ability to maintain a constructive mindset. To navigate these trials with resilience, believers must cultivate a robust mental fortitude grounded in the transformative principles of Scripture.

The apostle James encourages believers to consider it pure joy when facing trials because the testing of faith develops perseverance (*hypomonē* ὑπομονή). Perseverance must finish its work so that one may be mature and complete, not lacking anything (James 1:2-4). This maturation process necessitates a steadfastness of mind, a mental endurance that holds fast to biblical truths despite the emotional turbulence that trials may bring.

Engaging the Mind with the Psalms of Lament

The Psalms offer a profound model for engaging with emotional distress. Many of these ancient songs are laments that express deep sorrow, fear, and even anger. Yet, they do not remain in the depths of despair. Rather, they transition from a raw outpouring of emotion to a reaffirmation of trust in God's character and promises. For instance, Psalm 42 expresses a soul's deep thirst for God amidst tears and turmoil. The psalmist asks, "Why are you cast down, O my soul, and why are you in turmoil within me?" Yet, he answers his own despair with hope, "Hope in God; for I shall again praise him, my salvation" (Psalm 42:5). Through this dialogue, the psalmist demonstrates the process of taking captive every thought to make it obedient to Christ (*Christo hypotassō* Χριστῷ ὑποτάσσω), as Paul urges in 2 Corinthians 10:5.

The Preeminence of Christ in Mental Endurance

In maintaining mental fortitude, the supremacy of Christ over every aspect of life is paramount. Colossians 1:17 declares that in Him all things hold together. This truth implies that Christ is not only the sustainer of the physical universe but also the anchor for the believer's mental and emotional world. His preeminence assures believers that no trial is beyond His sovereign purview and, therefore, no thought need spiral into hopelessness. The Greek term for "hold together" (*sunistēmi* συνίστημι) suggests a cohesive force, a divine glue that maintains order amidst chaos. In times of trial, believers are reminded to fix their eyes on Jesus, the author, and perfecter of faith, who for the joy set before Him endured the cross (*hypomenō* ὑπομένω, endured), scorning its shame (Hebrews 12:2). This enduring is a model for believers to imitate, knowing that the trials they face are neither meaningless nor endless.

The Prophet Jeremiah's Example of Mental Resilience

Jeremiah, known as the weeping prophet, faced intense persecution and emotional anguish. Yet, amidst his laments, he also proclaimed truths that fortified his resolve. He declared, "The steadfast love of Jehovah never ceases; his mercies never come to an end; they are new every morning; great is your faithfulness" (Lamentations 3:22-23). In the Hebrew text, *chesed* (חֶסֶד, steadfast love) conveys a sense of lovingkindness that is not merely emotional but covenantal and action-oriented. Jeremiah's focus on Jehovah's unchanging character provided him with a solid foundation to withstand the fluctuating circumstances of life.

The Symbiotic Relationship Between Thought and Community

It is important to recognize that mental fortitude is not a solitary endeavor. The early church demonstrated a symbiotic relationship where believers' minds were sharpened by one another. Acts 2:42-47 depicts a community devoted to the apostles' teaching, fellowship, breaking of bread, and prayers. This communal aspect is crucial, for it allows believers to draw strength from one another during times of trial. The Greek word for fellowship (*koinōnia* κοινωνία) implies a deep sharing, a mutual participation that extends to emotional and mental support. When one member struggles with destructive thoughts, the community rallies to uphold, encourage, and redirect the focus toward the truth of God's Word.

The Imperative of Continuous Prayer

Philippians 4:6-7 emphasizes the importance of prayer in dealing with anxiety: "Do not be anxious about anything, but in everything by prayer and supplication with thanksgiving let your requests be made known to God." Prayer (*proseuchē* προσευχή) in this context is not a last resort but a first response to the onset of destructive thoughts. It is the conduit through which the peace of God, which surpasses all understanding, guards the hearts and minds of believers in Christ Jesus. This guarding (*phroureō* φρουρέω) is akin to a military sentinel, providing a protective custody over the believer's inner world.

Conforming to the Mind of Christ

To conform one's mind to that of Christ is to embrace a perspective that transcends earthly trials. Paul's exhortation in Romans 12:2 to be transformed by the renewal of the mind (*nous* νοῦς) is a call to an ongoing, active process. This transformation (*metamorphoō* μεταμορφόω) is not a one-time event but a continuous shaping and refining of thoughts and attitudes in the likeness of Christ's mind. The mind of Christ is characterized by obedience, servanthood, and sacrifice—attributes that equip believers to withstand trials with grace and perseverance.

In facing the trials of life, believers are not left to their own devices. The biblical approach to maintaining mental fortitude is comprehensive, engaging the whole person in a dynamic interplay between individual responsibility and communal support. It is rooted in the eternal truths of Scripture, the power of prayer, the example of Christ, and the sustaining fellowship of the body of Christ. Through these means, destructive thoughts are not merely suppressed but transformed, enabling believers to triumph in the battle for the Christian mind.

Edward D. Andrews

CHAPTER 10 Get the Correct Mental Grasp

The Importance of Properly Understanding Scripture

In the quest for renewing the mind and aligning oneself with the mind of Christ, the proper understanding of Scripture is fundamental. The Scriptures are not simply ancient texts but the living Word of God, designed to penetrate the deepest recesses of the human heart and mind. This transformative power of Scripture is contingent upon an accurate and profound grasp of its message.

When examining the text of the Bible, it is crucial to approach it with an understanding that every word, every nuance, carries significant weight. The Hebrew term for "word," *davar* (דָּבָר), and the Greek term *logos* (λόγος) both reflect a concept of the word as embodying an active and dynamic presence. Hence, understanding Scripture is not merely an intellectual exercise but an encounter with the *davar* or *logos* of God, which has the power to discern thoughts and intentions (Hebrews 4:12).

The Hebrew Mindset and Biblical Understanding

The Hebrew mindset, as seen in the Old Testament, is not abstract or speculative but deeply practical, concrete, and communal. For instance, the Shema, found in Deuteronomy 6:4, "Hear, O Israel: Jehovah our God, Jehovah is one," employs the Hebrew verb *shema* (שְׁמַע), which means to hear, listen, and obey. This verse does not just assert a theological fact but calls for an active response—obedience reflecting understanding. Likewise, understanding Scripture calls for a response that goes beyond cognition to obedience and transformation of life.

The Greek Concept of Knowledge and Understanding

In the New Testament, written in Koine Greek, the word for "knowledge," *gnosis* (γνῶσις), often connotes more than mere intellectual assent. It involves a relational aspect, as in knowing a person, and by extension, God's character and will. Furthermore, the word for "understand," *suniemi* (συνίημι), implies a bringing together or comprehending in a holistic sense. When Jesus explained parables, He often ended with, "He who has ears to hear, let him hear," indicating that understanding is not only cognitive but also involves a willingness to hear and act (Matthew 11:15).

The Role of the Holy Spirit in Understanding Scripture

While it is clear from Scripture that there is no indwelling of the Holy Spirit that supernaturally imparts understanding, the role of the Spirit-inspired Word is undeniable. The Word, which is "God-breathed" (*theopneustos* θεόπνευστος), provides the wisdom and guidance necessary for understanding (2 Timothy 3:16). The counsel of the Holy Spirit comes through a diligent study of this Word, meditation on its truths, and application in life.

Contextual Analysis for Deeper Understanding

To correctly grasp biblical texts, one must delve into the historical and grammatical context. For instance, understanding the covenantal language used by the prophets and apostles, such as the term *berith* (בְּרִית) in Hebrew, which means covenant, helps in comprehending the nature of God's promises and His relationship with humanity. Similarly, analyzing Greek terms like *diatheke* (διαθήκη), also translated as covenant or testament, sheds light on the New Testament's presentation of Jesus as the mediator of a better covenant (Hebrews 9:15).

Avoiding Eisegesis and Embracing Exegesis

One of the key aspects of correctly understanding Scripture is avoiding eisegesis, which is the imposition of one's own presuppositions, agendas, or biases into the text. Instead, exegesis must be employed, which is the careful drawing out of the text's true meaning according to its original context and intended audience. This distinction is critical because eisegesis can lead to misinterpretation and misapplication, whereas exegesis respects the integrity of the biblical message.

The Progressive Complexity in Understanding Scripture

The journey of understanding Scripture is progressive, moving from the simple to the complex, much like the Hebrew educational method of moving from the milk of the Word to solid food (Hebrews 5:12-14). This implies that believers are to grow in their ability to handle the Word of God, which requires time, effort, and spiritual maturity. As with the Bereans, who were commended for their noble character in searching the Scriptures daily to see if what Paul said was true (Acts 17:11), a mature believer critically examines and discerns the truths of Scripture.

The Interplay Between Individual Study and Corporate Understanding

While individual study of Scripture is important, the corporate aspect of understanding is also crucial. The early church's engagement with Scripture was often communal, with letters and gospels being read aloud in gatherings. This communal aspect allowed for mutual edification and the sharing of insights under the guidance of the Spirit-inspired Word, fostering a unified understanding among believers.

Properly understanding Scripture is not just about intellectual knowledge but about transformation. It is about allowing the Word of God to reshape one's thinking, values, and actions in alignment with the mind of Christ. It is about moving from a position of inherent mental bent towards evil to one of being conformed to the image of Christ. This journey requires the humble acknowledgment of our limitations, the commitment to study diligently, and the willingness to apply the truths of Scripture to our lives, both individually and communally. Through this process, believers are equipped to combat the strongholds that oppose the knowledge of God and are empowered to live in the victory that comes from a renewed mind.

Tools and Techniques for Accurate Biblical Interpretation

Accurate biblical interpretation is the cornerstone of developing a correct mental grasp of Scripture, which in turn is critical for the transformation of the Christian mind. To interpret the Bible accurately, several tools and techniques must be employed diligently and systematically. This not only ensures a deep understanding but also safeguards against misinterpretation, which can lead to doctrinal errors and hinder the believer's spiritual growth.

Understanding Language and Grammar

One of the foundational tools for biblical interpretation is a sound understanding of the original languages, Hebrew for the Old Testament and Greek for the New Testament. Each language carries its unique idioms, nuances, and grammatical structures that can significantly affect interpretation. For instance, the Hebrew word *chesed* (חֶסֶד) often translated as "lovingkindness" or "steadfast love," conveys a rich tapestry of loyalty, love, and mercy that is foundational to God's covenantal relationship with His people. Similarly, the Greek word *agape* (ἀγάπη) is often translated as "love," but it specifically refers to a selfless, sacrificial love that is central to the character of God and the attitude believers are to have toward one another.

Historical and Cultural Context

Understanding the historical and cultural context of the biblical text is imperative. The Bible was written in a world very different from our own, and without grasping the social, political, and religious dynamics of the time, one can easily misinterpret the text. For example, when Paul speaks to the Ephesian husbands to love their wives as Christ loved the church (Ephesians 5:25), understanding the patriarchal structure of ancient society can illuminate the radical nature of Paul's instruction.

Literary Genre and Analysis

The Bible contains various literary genres—narrative, poetry, wisdom literature, prophecy, epistles, and apocalyptic writings. Each genre has its conventions and must be interpreted accordingly. For example, the apocalyptic imagery found in Revelation is rich with symbolism and should not be interpreted with the same literal approach as the historical accounts in the book of Acts.

Contextual Reading

A verse or passage must always be interpreted in its immediate context as well as within the broader context of the chapter, book, and ultimately, the entire Bible. Isolation of verses can lead to *eisegesis*, or reading one's own ideas into the text. For instance, *Philippians 4:13*, "I can do all things through Christ who strengthens me," within its context, is about Paul speaking to being content in all circumstances, not a blanket statement for achieving any desired outcome.

Exegetical Precision

Exegetical precision involves a meticulous approach to the text, analyzing words, phrases, and syntactical structures. For example, the Greek word *dikaiosune* (δικαιοσύνη), often translated as "righteousness," carries legal connotations of justice, as well as relational aspects pertaining to character. Understanding its use in a particular passage requires examining its immediate literary context and comparing it with other occurrences in Scripture.

Use of Concordances and Lexicons

Concordances and lexicons are invaluable tools for studying the frequency and usage of words in their original languages. A lexicon can provide the range of meanings for a Hebrew or Greek word, while a concordance can show where the word appears throughout the Bible, which aids in understanding its nuances.

Consultation of Commentaries

While conservative in our theological outlook, it is wise to consult a range of commentaries, particularly those that adhere to a literal interpretation of Scripture. Commentaries can offer insights into difficult passages and provide historical background, alternative interpretations, and applications. However, discernment is necessary to ensure these insights align with sound doctrine.

Theological Framework

Interpretation must be consistent with the overall theological framework of Scripture. Doctrines such as the deity of Christ, salvation by faith, and the resurrection must inform our interpretation of specific passages. When examining a passage like *Romans 9:5*, where Paul speaks of the Christ who is "God over all, blessed forever," it must be interpreted in light of the full testimony of Scripture regarding the nature of Christ.

Integration of Doctrine and Practice

Accurate interpretation is not only about understanding what the text says but also about integrating its teachings into one's life. For example, James 1:22 admonishes believers to be doers of the word and not hearers only. This implies that the interpretation of Scripture should lead to practical application. When we come across imperatives in the Greek New Testament, such as *agapate* (ἀγαπᾶτε), "love," from John 13:34, it's not just an emotional suggestion but a command for action that should manifest in the believer's behavior.

Recognition of Progressive Revelation

The principle of progressive revelation acknowledges that Jehovah has gradually revealed His will and purposes over time. Earlier scriptural texts may contain shadows and types that are fulfilled in later revelations. For instance, the sacrificial system outlined in Leviticus finds its fulfillment in the atoning work of Christ, as explained in the book of Hebrews. Understanding this progressive nature is key to grasping the full meaning of biblical texts.

Avoidance of Allegory and Typology

While the Bible contains typology, an overemphasis on allegorical interpretations can obscure the plain meaning of the text. Allegory should only be employed when the text itself indicates it (as in Galatians 4:24), and even then, it should not override the primary, literal meaning. An understanding that sticks closely to the text ensures that interpretations remain grounded in the intended message of Scripture.

Distinguishing Between Prescriptive and Descriptive Texts

It is crucial to distinguish between what Scripture describes and what it prescribes. Descriptive texts relay what happened, such as David's actions in the historical books. Prescriptive texts, like the commands found in the Pauline epistles, instruct believers on how they should live. Failing to distinguish between the two can lead to misapplication of biblical narratives.

Use of Cross-References

Cross-referencing scripture with scripture is an effective technique for interpretation, as the best interpreter of the Bible is the Bible itself. For example, understanding Jehovah's promise to Abraham in Genesis 12 can be enhanced by looking at how the New

Testament writers refer to this promise and its fulfillment through Christ.

Role of Prayer and Dependence on Jehovah

While the Holy Spirit does not indwell believers, prayer remains a vital tool for seekers of truth. Approaching the study of Scripture with prayer is a way of expressing dependence on Jehovah for wisdom and understanding. James 1:5 encourages believers to ask God for wisdom, which He gives generously to those who seek it.

Humility and Teachability

A correct mental grasp of Scripture cannot be achieved without a humble and teachable spirit. Recognizing our propensity for error and the need for correction aligns with the wisdom found in Proverbs, where the fear of Jehovah is the beginning of knowledge (Proverbs 1:7). Teachability allows for growth in understanding and guards against the arrogance that can lead to doctrinal rigidity and error.

Community of Faith

Engaging with a community of faith provides a context for discussion, correction, and sharpening of interpretation. As Proverbs 27:17 states, "Iron sharpens iron, and one man sharpens another." This communal aspect of interpretation helps to ensure that personal biases are challenged and that a plurality of insights is considered.

Synthesis and Coherence

Finally, accurate biblical interpretation seeks to synthesize the whole counsel of God into a coherent understanding that respects the diversity of Scripture while maintaining its unity. The Bible does not contradict itself; apparent discrepancies often reveal a deeper harmony when carefully studied. For example, Paul's teachings on justification by faith are not at odds with James's emphasis on faith and works; instead, they present a coherent doctrine of faith that is alive and active.

By employing these tools and techniques with dedication and reverence, believers can attain a more profound and accurate grasp of biblical truth. Such a grasp is not merely academic but transformational, equipping believers to renew their minds and align themselves with the mind of Christ, ultimately enabling them to engage in the battle for the Christian mind with the full armor of God's Word.

Common Misconceptions and How to Avoid Them

In the quest for a correct mental grasp of Scripture, various misconceptions can impede understanding and lead to misinterpretation. Recognizing and avoiding these errors is crucial for anyone seeking to engage deeply with the Word of God and apply its wisdom effectively.

One prevalent misconception is the notion of *scriptura sub cultura*, the idea that Scripture should be read and understood primarily through the lens of contemporary culture. This approach can lead to an anachronistic interpretation, where modern ideas and values are projected onto the text, skewing its original meaning. For instance, the concept of equality is viewed differently today than in the time of the New Testament. While today it may imply absolute uniformity in roles and functions, in *Galatians 3:28*, the apostle Paul's assertion that there is neither Jew nor Greek, slave nor free, male nor female, is rooted in the shared status of believers as heirs according to the promise. This does not erase functional distinctions but underscores unity in salvation.

Another common error is *eisegesis*, where one's personal opinions or beliefs are read into the text, rather than drawing out the text's true message (*exegesis*). For example, when examining Jehovah's promise to never destroy the earth again with a flood in *Genesis 9:11*, reading into this a guarantee against all forms of global catastrophe imposes an unwarranted assurance that goes beyond the scope of the covenant with Noah.

A third misconception involves the confusion between prescriptive and descriptive passages. Some readers fail to discern whether a text is prescribing what should be done or merely describing what has occurred. The narrative of David and Bathsheba in 2 Samuel 11 is descriptive, recounting historical events, and does not prescribe moral approval of David's actions.

The literalist trap, or the insistence on a strictly literal interpretation of all scriptural elements regardless of genre, is yet another misunderstanding. The Psalms, for example, are replete with poetic language, such as in *Psalm 91:4*, where it is said that Jehovah will cover you with His feathers. Understanding the metaphorical language is crucial to grasping the psalmist's intention to convey God's protective care, not a physical attribute of deity.

Conversely, some readers might fall into an allegorical excess, where they attempt to find hidden meanings behind every text, often at the expense of the clear and plain meaning. Paul's mention of the armor of God in *Ephesians 6:11-17* is not an invitation to find esoteric spiritual truths behind each piece of armor but a call to understand the spiritual realities of the believer's battle against sin and Satan.

The pitfall of proof-texting is another significant challenge. This practice involves taking verses out of their context to support a particular view. When Paul speaks of Jehovah creating from one man every nation of mankind in *Acts 17:26*, using this verse to support racial equality is valid, but one must not neglect the surrounding context which emphasizes God's sovereignty in determining allotted periods and boundaries of dwelling.

The misconception of the "clear text" can lead to an oversimplification of interpretation. Some may claim that the meaning of Scripture is always evident at face value, dismissing the complexities inherent in the text. For example, Jehovah's declaration in *Isaiah 55:8* that His thoughts are not our thoughts can be too simplistically interpreted as an impenetrable divide between God and humanity, ignoring the fact that the same passage invites us to seek Jehovah while He may be found.

There is also the fallacy of the self-sufficient reader, where one believes they can understand the Bible entirely on their own, neglecting the value of historical insight, scholarship, and the Christian community. Interpreting *2 Timothy 3:16*, where all Scripture is stated to be inspired by God and profitable for teaching, as a call to solitary interpretation neglects the communal aspect of discernment and the guidance that comes from the collective body of Christ.

To avoid these misconceptions, one must approach Scripture with a balance of reverence for its divine inspiration and recognition of its human authorship within historical and cultural contexts. Embracing a *sola scriptura* approach, where Scripture interprets Scripture, can prevent many of the errors that stem from imposing external frameworks onto the biblical text.

When encountering challenging passages, it is wise to consult multiple translations, lexicons, and concordances, which provide insight into the original languages. The Hebrew term *hesed* (חֶסֶד), often translated as "steadfast love," conveys rich nuances that single English words cannot capture. Similarly, the Greek word *sarx* (σάρξ), typically translated as "flesh," has a range of meanings from the physical flesh to the sinful nature of humans, understanding which requires careful scriptural comparison and analysis.

Furthermore, one must diligently differentiate between literal and metaphorical language, historical and didactic passages, and prescriptive versus descriptive texts. Prayerful study, a humble attitude, and a willingness to be corrected will safeguard against the prideful assumption that one's understanding is infallible.

Finally, engaging with the wider body of believers, respecting the interpretative work of faithful scholars, and considering the historical testimony of the church can provide a well-rounded and more accurate understanding of Scripture. This communal aspect is instrumental in attaining a correct mental grasp of biblical truths, as the Spirit of God has been at work throughout the history of the church, guiding His people into all truth.

The Role of Diligence and Prayer in Gaining Insight

In the sacred quest for understanding the Scriptures, diligence and prayer are indispensable tools that can shape and align the believer's mind with the profound truths of God's Word. The journey to acquiring a correct mental grasp of biblical knowledge is not a passive one; it requires active pursuit and the assistance of God through prayerful reflection.

Diligence: The Pursuit of Understanding

Diligence in the study of Scripture involves a persistent and methodical approach to learning. The Bereans are a prime example of such diligence; they examined the Scriptures daily to see if what Paul said was true (*Acts 17:11*). This kind of scrutiny involves diving into the original language, context, and culture of the biblical text. The Hebrew term *yada* (ידע) and the Greek *ginosko* (γινώσκω) both translated as "to know," imply an experiential, intimate knowledge, not just a factual acquaintance. To know God and His statutes in this way is to let the Word dwell richly within, guiding and transforming one's thoughts and actions (*Colossians 3:16*).

For the Christian mind, diligence means not just reading but studying Scripture with the intent to apply it. In the Greek, the term *spoudazo* (σπουδάζω), often translated as "be diligent," carries the sense of making haste, being eager, and exerting oneself. It implies an earnest effort to rightly divide the word of truth, which Paul urged Timothy to do (*2 Timothy 2:15*). This correct handling of the Word requires not just reading the text but dissecting it, understanding the nuances of words like *agape* (ἀγάπη) – the selfless, sacrificial love – which defines how believers are to relate to one another.

The diligent student of the Bible must also grasp the interconnectedness of Scripture. For instance, the theme of redemption found in the account of the Passover lamb in *Exodus 12* is a shadow of the ultimate sacrifice of Christ, the Lamb of God, in the

New Testament (*John 1:29*). Such typological understanding requires a depth of study that goes beyond surface reading.

Prayer: The Divine Conversation

Prayer is the means by which believers engage in a divine conversation, seeking wisdom that is not of this age. James, the brother of Jesus, assured believers that if any lacked wisdom, they should ask God, who gives generously to all without reproach, and it will be given to them (*James 1:5*). Prayer is not a mere ritual but a lifeline to the Father, who illuminates the text and makes it alive in the believer's heart.

In prayer, the believer can echo the Psalmist's cry: "Open my eyes, that I may behold wondrous things out of your law" (*Psalm 119:18*). This is not a passive request but an active seeking of divine insight that acknowledges God's role in spiritual enlightenment. When studying the concept of faith, for instance, the Greek word *pistis* (πίστις) encompasses trust, belief, and faithfulness. Understanding *pistis* in its full biblical context requires the Spirit's guidance to go beyond mere intellectual agreement to a firm conviction that shapes one's very being.

Prayer is also the believer's recourse in combating the spiritual warfare that threatens to distort or suppress the truth. Paul recognized that the struggle was not against flesh and blood but against the spiritual forces of evil in the heavenly places (*Ephesians 6:12*). Therefore, the prayer of the believer is not only for personal insight but also for the strength to withstand doctrinal error and the deceptive schemes of the adversary.

Integration of Diligence and Prayer

The integration of diligence and prayer leads to a holistic approach to Scripture, one that honors God by striving for accuracy in understanding while humbly relying on divine assistance. The process of transformation that Paul speaks of in *Romans 12:2* involves both the renewing of the mind—a cognitive restructuring through the intake and application of God's Word—and the supplication for divine guidance to discern the perfect will of God.

In the historical-grammatical method of interpretation, this integrated approach respects the text's historical context, its grammatical construction, and its canonical form, while prayerfully seeking the Spirit's guidance in application. The *kerygma* (κήρυγμα) – the proclamation of the gospel message – becomes not just a historical fact to be studied but a transformative truth to be embraced.

As Christians endeavor to navigate the complexities of hermeneutics, the nuances of biblical languages, and the depths of theological doctrines, the twin disciplines of diligence and prayer become their stalwart companions. Like the two cherubim that overshadowed the mercy seat in the Holy of Holies (*Exodus 25:20*), these disciplines protectively hover over the mind of the believer, guiding them into all truth (*John 16:13*).

Conclusion: The Path to True Insight

The role of diligence and prayer in gaining insight is a testament to the partnership between human responsibility and divine enablement. The journey to a correct mental grasp of the Scriptures is one that is intensely personal, yet universally commanded for all believers. It is through these means that the mind is prepared for the battle, armed with the full armor of God, ready to take every thought captive to obey Christ (*2 Corinthians 10:5*). It is a lifelong pursuit, yet one that promises the incomparable reward of knowing God and being transformed into the likeness of His Son. In this divine-human cooperation lies the essence of true biblical scholarship and the heart of the Christian mind.

CHAPTER 11 How Are We to Understand the Indwelling of the Holy Spirit?

A Clarification of Terms: What Does "Indwelling" Really Mean?

In theological discourse, especially when considering the doctrine of the Holy Spirit's work within the believer, the term "indwelling" frequently surfaces. To speak exhaustively on this topic, we must carefully parse the term and explore its scriptural usage and implications. The concept of the Holy Spirit's indwelling is often associated with the Spirit's personal and persistent presence within the Christian. However, in the framework of the book "The Battle for the Christian Mind," the perspective taken is distinct from traditional views that posit a literal indwelling of the Holy Spirit.

The Nature of "Indwelling"

In the New Testament, the Greek word *enoikeo* (ἐνοικέω), often translated as "dwell," signifies to inhabit or to live in. When the Scriptures speak of the Spirit that "dwells" in you (*Romans 8:11*), the term must be understood within the broader biblical context. The key is to consider *enoikeo* in a metaphorical sense, describing the influence and operational presence of the Spirit through the Word of God that resides in the hearts and minds of believers.

The Holy Spirit's Operational Presence

The Holy Spirit's presence is made manifest in the life of a Christian through the transformative power of the Word of God. This Word is described as living and active (*Hebrews 4:12*), having the divine *dunamis* (δύναμις) to change the inner person. Thus, when believers study and apply Scripture, they exhibit the fruit of the Spirit, which is, in essence, the outcome of God's teachings taking root in their lives.

The Influence of the Spirit through the Word

In this view, the Spirit "indwells" the Christian in the sense that the teachings and guidance of the Spirit, as found in the Bible, profoundly influence the believer's thoughts, actions, and decisions. The inspired Scriptures are the vehicle through which the Holy Spirit operates. It's not that the Spirit physically occupies the believer, but rather that the believer's consistent immersion in the Word molds the individual's character and conduct to reflect Christ-like qualities.

Understanding through Embracing Truth

The apostle Paul presents a nuanced understanding of how we comprehend spiritual truths. In *1 Corinthians 2:12-14*, he differentiates between mere intellectual acknowledgment and an embracing of these truths as valuable and applicable. This embracing is what it means to have a spiritual understanding, which is more than just mental ascent— it's an internalization that influences one's worldview and behavior.

Contrast with Physical Indwelling

In contrast to some traditional teachings, the non-literal indwelling emphasizes that there is no physical entity of the Holy Spirit residing within people. Instead, the Holy Spirit's work is recognized in how the believer's life evidences the wisdom, power, and fruit of the teachings of Scripture. It's through this Spirit-infused wisdom that Christians can discern and dismantle the corrupt thoughts and philosophies that oppose God's truth (*2 Corinthians 10:4-5*).

The Role of the Conscience

The conscience, an innate sense of right and wrong given by God, is heightened and sharpened through interaction with the Holy Spirit's teachings. It is through the conscientious application of the Word that a believer is guided, rather than through a mystical indwelling presence.

A well-nurtured conscience, informed by the deep truths of Scripture, aids the believer in the battle for the mind, helping to align one's thoughts with the divine will.

The Transformative Impact on the Christian Mind

The indwelling of the Holy Spirit, understood as the influence of God's Word, is integral to the transformation Paul speaks of in *Romans 12:2*. As believers continually feed on the Scriptures, they are transformed by renewing their minds, which leads to a demonstrable change in how they live and think. It is not a passive change but an active reprogramming of the mind to think biblically, to weigh every idea and thought against the truths of Scripture.

Conclusion: The Mind Guided by the Word

The indwelling of the Holy Spirit is thus a metaphorical concept pointing to the profound and ongoing influence of God's Word in the life of a believer. The Scriptures, being God-breathed (*2 Timothy 3:16*), are the Holy Spirit's instrument to teach, rebuke, correct, and train in righteousness. This divine influence brings about a mental and spiritual renewal that aligns the Christian's thoughts with God's truth, empowering the believer to stand firm against the onslaughts of false reasoning and secular ideologies.

The book "The Battle for the Christian Mind" seeks to dispel misconceptions about the indwelling of the Holy Spirit, instead highlighting the significance of the Spirit-inspired Word as the primary means by which God guides and transforms the believer. It is through a deep engagement with this Word that the Christian is equipped to combat the pervasive influence of sin and error, fostering a robust and resilient Christian mind.

The Holy Spirit's Role in Understanding and Applying Scripture

In the sphere of Christian thought, the role of the Holy Spirit in the comprehension and application of Scripture is a subject of profound depth. Within the framework of *The Battle for the Christian Mind*, it is crucial to establish that while the indwelling of the Holy Spirit is not a physical presence within us, the Spirit's influence is pivotal in illuminating Scripture and empowering believers to integrate its truths into their lives.

Understanding Scripture Through the Spirit's Influence

In the original languages of Scripture, the New Testament Greek provides us with a nuanced term: *nous* (νοῦς). This word often refers to the mind or understanding, and is particularly enlightening when considering the Holy Spirit's role in the believer's comprehension of Scripture. The *nous* is not merely an organ of intellectual apprehension but the center of spiritual discernment. When Paul speaks of a renewal of the *nous* in *Romans 12:2*, he is talking about a transformation that affects not just the intellectual grasp of Scripture but its application to the believer's life.

This renewal of the mind, this *anakainosis tou noos* (ἀνακαίνωσις τοῦ νοός), is a pivotal aspect of understanding Scripture. It involves a transformation that allows a person to perceive and apply God's word in a way that goes beyond academic understanding to a profound, personal insight. This is not due to the physical indwelling of the Holy Spirit but rather the Spirit's influence through the teachings and principles found within the Bible.

Applying Scripture with the Mind of Christ

Embracing the truths of Scripture as meaningful and relevant is central to the Christian experience. This is an active, ongoing process of applying biblical principles to everyday life. The *phronema tou Christou* (φρόνημα τοῦ Χριστοῦ), or the mind of Christ, is an essential element for the believer, as highlighted in *1 Corinthians 2:16*. Having the mind of Christ means adopting His attitudes and responses as one's own, thus shaping one's worldview and decision-making process according to the moral and spiritual truths found in the Bible.

The influence of the Holy Spirit in this respect is critical. While the Spirit does not indwell believers in a physical sense, the Spirit-inspired Word of God is instrumental in shaping and refining the believer's conscience. This refined conscience then becomes a vital tool in making decisions that reflect the will of God. As believers engage with Scripture, they are not merely learning data; they are having their very thought processes and attitudes shaped by the divine perspective.

The Transformative Power of Scripture

The transformative power of Scripture, *dunamis* (δύναμις), is evident as believers encounter the living Word of God and allow it to work within their hearts. This is not a passive reception but an active engagement with the text. For example, the *paraklēsis* (παράκλησις) and *oikodome* (οἰκοδομή) found in the pages of Scripture—comfort and edification—become practical realities as believers apply the principles to their lives and experience growth and encouragement.

The application of Scripture under the guidance of the Holy Spirit leads to the *katharsis* (κάθαρσις), or purification, of the mind and heart. This purification is a cleansing of the old, sinful ways of thinking and adopting a new, godly perspective. This process is reflected in the life of the believer as a progressive sanctification, a setting apart for God's purposes.

Discernment and the Holy Spirit

Discernment, or *diakrisis* (διάκρισις), plays a significant role in understanding and applying Scripture. The Holy Spirit, through the Word, provides the believer with the capacity to distinguish between truth and error, between what is spiritually beneficial and what is not.

The book of Hebrews (*Hebrews 5:14*) speaks about mature believers having their senses trained to discern good and evil. This training comes through a consistent and prayerful engagement with Scripture, allowing the principles taught to sift through thoughts and intentions, thereby equipping believers to make godly choices.

Overcoming Mental Strongholds

The battle for the Christian mind is a battle against mental strongholds. These are patterns of thinking that stand in opposition to the knowledge of God. Through the application of Scripture, empowered by the Spirit's influence, believers are able to *kathairein* (καθαιρεῖν), or tear down, these strongholds. The Holy Spirit's role is to shine a light on these areas through the Word, to convict and to challenge believers to align their thinking with biblical truths.

In conclusion, the Holy Spirit's role in the understanding and application of Scripture is not a matter of physical indwelling but a powerful influence exerted through the Word of God. This divine influence acts upon the *nous*, enabling believers to perceive, understand, and apply Scripture in a way that goes beyond the intellect, transforming the heart and mind to reflect the mind of Christ. It is this process that equips believers to stand firm in the battle for the Christian mind, holding fast to the truths of Scripture against the onslaught of worldly philosophies and spiritual deceptions.

The Misinterpretation of 1 Corinthians 2:12-14 and Its Clarification

The text of *1 Corinthians 2:12-14* has been the bedrock for many discussions about the role of the Holy Spirit in the life of believers. Paul's words here are often cited to support the view that the Holy Spirit indwells the believer in a way that is almost mystical, providing direct insight into spiritual truths that are otherwise inaccessible to the human mind. However, a careful examination of the text within the original Greek language, the broader Pauline corpus, and the entire

Biblical narrative reveals a different perspective that aligns with a conservative, literal interpretation of Scripture.

Understanding the Terms

In *1 Corinthians 2:12*, we read, "Now we have received, not the spirit of the world, but the spirit which is of God; that we might know the things that are freely given to us of God." The Greek word translated as "know" here is *ginōskomen* (γινώσκομεν), indicating a form of knowledge that goes beyond mere intellectual ascent. This knowing is experiential and relational. It suggests that through the teachings and influence of the Holy Spirit as found in the Scriptures, we become aware of the blessings bestowed upon us by Jehovah.

Continuing to verse 13, Paul clarifies that the words they speak are "not in the words which man's wisdom teacheth, but which the Holy Ghost teacheth; comparing spiritual things with spiritual." The verb "teacheth" here is *didaskō* (διδάσκω), reinforcing the idea that the Holy Spirit's role is that of a teacher through the medium of the inspired Scriptures. This teaching is not through mystical means but through the spiritual understanding one gains from engaging deeply with the Word of God.

In verse 14, the Apostle describes a person who does not accept the things of the Spirit of God, for they are *mōria* (μωρία) to him, meaning "foolishness," and he cannot understand them because they are spiritually discerned. The term "understand" (*ginōskei*, γινώσκει) here has a judicial sense, meaning to come to know, recognize, or discern. This is not a lack of intellectual capability but rather a volitional rejection of God's revelation, not due to a deficiency in mental capacity but in spiritual disposition.

The Contextual Clarification

Paul's argument is not that the unbeliever lacks the intellectual ability to understand the Scripture but that there is a lack of spiritual receptivity and appreciation for the truths of God. This distinction is crucial. The "natural man" (*psychikos*, ψυχικός) as mentioned in *1 Corinthians 2:14* does not refer to a person without the Holy Spirit within them but rather someone operating purely from a human point of view—limited to human wisdom without the insights that come from a scripturally informed understanding.

The Role of the Spirit in Understanding

While the Holy Spirit is not physically indwelling the believer, His influence is exerted through the inspired words of Scripture. When believers read the Bible, they are not merely engaging with ink on paper but with the *rhēma* (ῥῆμα), the uttered word of God, which is alive and active (*Hebrews 4:12*). It is through the Scriptures that the Spirit "teaches," illuminating the truths contained therein and helping believers to apply these truths in their lives.

Scripture Interpreting Scripture

A key to understanding *1 Corinthians 2:12-14* is found within the principle of "scripture interpreting scripture." When the Holy Spirit "teaches," it is not through imparting secret knowledge or private interpretations but through enabling believers to understand one part of Scripture in light of another. This principle is *analogia scripturae*—the harmony of Scripture. The insights gained from this process do not come from an esoteric indwelling but from the consistent study and application of the Word.

The Influence of the Spirit and the Renewal of the Mind

The true battle for the Christian mind is not in seeking mystical experiences of the Spirit but in the continual renewal of the mind (*anakainōsis tou noos*, ἀνακαίνωσις τοῦ νοός) as commanded in *Romans 12:2*. This renewal comes through the Spirit's influence as we immerse ourselves in Scripture. As our minds are saturated with biblical truth, our thinking is transformed, and we start to develop the mind of Christ (*phronēma tou Christou*, φρόνημα τοῦ Χριστοῦ) described in *1 Corinthians 2:16*.

Conclusion: Embracing Spiritual Truths

In conclusion, the indwelling of the Holy Spirit as traditionally understood is not a requirement for understanding spiritual truths. Instead, it is through the consistent, prayerful study of God's Word that believers are equipped to discern and embrace these truths. The Spirit's role is one of influence and illumination through the Scriptures, not physical indwelling, empowering believers to renew their minds and thereby engage in the battle for the Christian mind with the mighty spiritual weapons that God provides.

Embracing Biblical Truths Without the Concept of the Indwelling of the Holy Spirit

The concept of the Holy Spirit "indwelling" within the believer has long been a topic of extensive theological debate. Central to understanding this concept from a biblical perspective is to return to the foundational truths of Scripture, examining what the Bible really says about the interaction between the Holy Spirit and the believer's mind. This examination is critical because the mind is the battlefield where truth and error wrestle, and where the victory for one's spiritual life is often determined.

The Mind in Spiritual Warfare

Human nature, with its propensity towards evil as described in Genesis 6:5 and 8:21, and the heart's treacherous condition as in Jeremiah 17:9, sets the stage for a constant struggle within the mind of the believer. This struggle is not against flesh and blood but against spiritual forces that seek to corrupt and deceive (Ephesians 6:12). The Apostle Paul's exhortation to use spiritual weapons to destroy strongholds is a call to engage the mind with divine truth (2 Corinthians 10:4). The mind, therefore, must be fortified—not with mystical experiences or subjective feelings—but with the objective and authoritative Word of God.

The Word of God as the Sword of the Spirit

If the Holy Spirit does not indwell in a metaphysical sense, then how does He influence the believer? Ephesians 6:17 speaks of "the sword of the Spirit, which is the word of God." The Greek term *rhēma* (ῥῆμα) refers to the spoken word, and in this context, it signifies the Scriptures. Thus, it is through the engagement with the Scripture that the believer wields the spiritual sword, combating false ideologies and renewing the mind. The transformative process described in Romans 12:2 is not through an inward mystical force but through the *anakainōsis* (ἀνακαίνωσις) or renewal that comes from applying scriptural truths to one's thought life.

The Work of the Spirit Through the Word

The Holy Spirit's operation in the life of a believer is closely linked with the Word of God. As Jesus promised the Spirit would guide His followers into all truth (John 16:13), this guidance is understood as the Spirit working through the Scriptures to illuminate and apply the truths contained within them. The Greek word for "guide" in this passage is *hodegeō* (ὁδηγέω), which indicates leading along a path. The "path" here is not a mystical journey but a clear and discernible walk in the truths of Scripture.

Understanding vs. Embracing Spiritual Truths

First Corinthians 2:14 reveals that the person without the Spirit does not accept the things that come from the Spirit of God. The Greek phrase *ou dechetai* (οὐ δέχεται) implies a rejection, not an inability to intellectually comprehend. Therefore, it is not an indwelling Spirit that enables understanding but rather the teaching of the Scriptures that the Spirit has inspired. The words "understand" in this verse are derived from *ginōskei* (γινώσκει), indicating not just cognitive recognition but an embracing of these truths as valuable and relevant.

The Conscience and the Holy Spirit

The conscience, which is a God-given aspect of human awareness, needs to be informed and strengthened by the Word of God. The Holy

Spirit works in conjunction with the Word to convict the world concerning sin, righteousness, and judgment (John 16:8). The Greek term for "convict" is *elegchō* (ἐλέγχω), which means to expose or refute. The Spirit exposes the depths of human sin and the beauty of divine righteousness through the teachings of Scripture. A conscience that is aligned with the Word is sensitive and effective, whereas one that is ignored becomes calloused.

Unity of Mind and Lowliness of Mind

The call for unity among believers, as seen in Philippians 2:2, is not a mystical unity brought about by a nebulous force but a unity of mind (*phronēma* - φρόνημα) rooted in common adherence to biblical truth. Similarly, the lowliness of mind (*tapeinophrosynē* - ταπεινοφροσύνη) exhibited by Christ and His followers is a humility that comes from understanding one's position before God as revealed in the Scriptures, not from an inner spiritual revelation.

The Result of Embracing Biblical Truths

The outcome of embracing biblical truths is a life that is visibly transformed by the renewal of the mind. This transformation is a testimony to the power of the Word of God and the Spirit's influence through it. The Holy Spirit's role is not diminished by removing the concept of indwelling; rather, it is magnified as the believer sees the Spirit's power manifested through the concrete changes in their thinking and behavior as they align with Scripture.

Embracing biblical truths without the concept of the indwelling of the Holy Spirit places the focus squarely on the Scriptures as the means by which God communicates with and influences the believer. This perspective aligns with a conservative, historical-grammatical interpretation of the Bible, emphasizing the sufficiency of Scripture for all matters of faith and practice. It is within the sacred text that the Spirit's power is encountered, leading to a mind transformed by truth and a life reflective of the character of Christ.

Bibliography

Aitchison, J. (2007). *The Articulate Mammal: An Introduction to Psycholinguistics - Fifth Edition.* London: Routledge.

Akin, D. L. (2001). *The New American Commentary: 1, 2, 3 John.* Nashville, TN: Broadman & Holman .

Alden, R. L. (2001). *Job, The New American Commentary, vol. 11 .* Nashville: Broadman & Holman Publishers.

Anders, M. (1999). *Holman New Testament Commentary: vol. 8, Galatians-Colossians .* Nashville, TN: Broadman & Holman Publishers.

Anders, M. (1999). *Holman New Testament Commentary: vol. 8, Galatians, Ephesians, Philippians, Colossians.* Nashville, TN: Broadman & Holman Publishers.

Anders, M. (2005). *Holman Old Testament Commentary - Proverbs .* Nashville: B&H Publishing.

Anders, M., & Butler, T. (2002). *Holman Old Testament Commentary: Isaiah.* Nashiville, TN: B&H Publishing.

Anders, M., & Lawson, S. (2004). *Holman Old Testament Commentary - Psalms: 11.* Grand Rapids: B&H Publishing.

Anders, M., & McIntosh, D. (2009). *Holman Old Testament Commentary - Deuteronomy.* Nashville: B&H Publishing.

Anderson, N. T. (2003). *Discipleship Counseling: The Complete Guide to Helping Others: Walk in Freedom and Gow in Christ.* Ventura: Regal Books.

Andrews, E. D. (2015). *EVIDENCE THAT YOU ARE TRULY CHRISTIAN: Keep Testing Yourselves to See If You Are In the Faith - Keep Examining Yourselves.* Cambridge, OH: Christian Publishing House.

Andrews, E. D. (2016). *CHRISTIAN THEOLOGY: The Evangelism Study Tool.* Cambridge, OH: Christian Publishing House.

Andrews, E. D. (2016). *FOR AS I THINK IN MY HEART—SO I AM: Combining Biblical Counseling with Cognitive Behavioral Therapy [Second Edition].* Cambridge: Christian Publishing House.

Andrews, E. D. (2016). *YOUR WORD IS TRUTH: Being Sanctified In the Truth.* Cambridge, OH: Christian Publishing House.

Andrews, E. D. (2017). *HUMAN IMPERFECTION: While We Were Sinners Christ Died For Us.* Cambridge, OH: Christian Ppublishing House.

Andrews, E. D. (2017). *THE OUTSIDER: Coming-of-Age In This Moment.* Cambridge, OH: Christian Publishing House.

Andrews, E. D. (2017). *TURN OLD HABITS INTO NEW HABITS: Why and How the Bible Makes a Difference.* Cambridge, OH: Christian Publishing House.

Andrews, E. D. (2017). *YOU CAN MAKE A DIFFERENCE: Why and How Your Christian Life Makes a Difference.* Cambridge, OH: Christian Publishing House.

Andrews, E. D. (2018). *LET GOD USE YOU TO SOLVE YOUR PROBLEMS: GOD Will Instruct You and Teach You In the Way You Should Go.* Cambridge, OH: Christian Publishing House.

Andrews, E. D. (2018). *THE POWER OF GOD: The Word That Will Change Your Life Today.* Cambridge, OH: Christian Publishing House.

Andrews, E. D. (2018). *WHY ME?: When Bad Things Happen to Good People.* Cambridge, OH: Christian Publishing House.

Andrews, E. D. (2019). *SATAN: Know Your Enemy.* Cambridge, OH: Christian Publishing House.

Andrews, E. D. (2022). *THE LETTER OF JAMES: An Apologetic and Background Exposition of the Holy Scriptures (CPH New Testament Commentary).* Cambridge, Ohio: Christian Publishing House.

Andrews, E. D. (2023). *BIBLICAL EXEGESIS: Biblical Criticism on Trial.* Cambridge, OH: Christian Publishing House.

Andrews, E. D. (2023). *CHRISTIAN APOLOGETICS: Answering the Tough Questions: Evidence and Reason in Defense of the Faith.* Cambridge, Ohio: Christian Publishing House.

Andrews, E. D. (2023). *FAITHFUL MINDS: A Biblical and Cognitive Behavioral Therapy Approach to Mental Health and Wellness.* Cambridge, OH: Christian Publishing House.

Andrews, E. D. (2023). *LIFE DOES HAVE A PURPOSE: Discovering and Living Your Ultimate Purpose.* Cambridge, OH: Christian Publishing House.

Andrews, E. D. (2023). *MERE CHRISTIANITY REIMAGINED: Rediscovering the Faith for the 21st Century.* Cambridge, OH: Christian Publishing House.

Andrews, E. D. (2023). *THE BOOK OF PROVERBS Chapters 1-15: CPH Old Testament Commentary: Volume 17.* Cambridge, OH: Christian Publishing House.

Andrews, E. D. (2023). *THE BOOK OF PROVERBS Chapters 16-23: CPH Old Testament Commentary: Volume 18.* Cambridge, OH: Christian Publishing House.

Andrews, E. D. (2023). *THE EXPOSITORY DICTIONARY: A Companion Study Tool to the Updated American Standard Version.* Cambridge, OH: Christian Publishing House.

Andrews, E. D. (2023). *THE OLD TESTAMENT: Commentary, Background, & Bible Difficulties (Introduction to the Old Testament).* Cambridge, OH: Christian Publishing House.

Andrews, E. D. (2023). *UNSHAKABLE BELIEFS: Strategies for Strengthening and Defending Your Faith.* Cambridge, OH: Christian Publishing House.

Andrews, E. D., & Marshall, T. F. (2023). *PAUL'S LETTER TO THE EPHESIANS: CPH New Testament Commentary.* Cambridge, OH: Christian Publishing House.

Andrews, E. D., & Torrey, R. A. (2016). *Christian Living: How to Succeed in the Christian Life.* Cambridge, OH: Christian Publishing House.

Andrews, S. J., & Bergen, R. D. (2009). *Holman Old Testament Commentary: 1-2 Samuel.* Nashville: Broadman & Holman.

Backus, W. (2000). *What Your Counselor Never Told You.* Bloomington: Bethany House.

Balz, H., & Schneider, G. (1978). *Exegetical Dictionary of the New Testament.* Edinburgh: T & T Clark Ltd.

Barker, K. L., & Bailey, W. (2001). *The New American Commentary: vol. 20, Micah, Nahum, Habakkuk, Zephaniah.* Nashville, TN: Broadman & Holman Publishers.

Benner, D. G. (1992, 2003). *Strategic Pastoral Counseling: A Short-Term Structural Model.* Grand Rapids: Baker Academic.

Benner, D. G., & Hill, P. C. (1985, 1999). *Baker Encyclopedia of Psychology and Counseling (Second Edition).* Grand Rapids: Baker Books.

Bercot, D. W. (1998). *A Dictionary of Early Christian Beliefs.* Peabody: Hendrickson.

Bergen, R. D. (1996). *The New American Commentary: 1-2 Samuel.* Nashville: Broadman & Holman.

Blomberg, C. (1992). *The New American Commentary: Matthew.* Nashville, TN: Broadman & Holman Publishers.

Boa, K., & Kruidenier, W. (2000). *Holman New Testament Commentary: Romans.* Nashville: Broadman & Holman.

Borchert, G. L. (2001). *The New American Commentary: John 1-11 .* Nashville, TN: Broadman & Holman Publishers.

Borchert, G. L. (2002). *The New American Commentary vol. 25B, John 12–21.* Nashville: Broadman & Holman Publishers.

Brand, C., Draper, C., & Archie, E. (2003). *Holman Illustrated Bible Dictionary: Revised, Updated and Expanded.* Nashville, TN: Holman.

Breneman, M. (1993). *The New American Commentary, vol. 10, Ezra, Nehemiah, Esther.* Nashville: Broadman & Holman Publishers.

Bromiley, G. W., & Friedrich, G. (1964-). *Theological Dictionary of the New Testament, ed. Gerhard Kittel, vol. 4.* Grand Rapids, MI: Eerdmans.

Brooks, J. A. (1992). *The New American Commentary: Mark (Volume 23).* Nashville: Broadman & Holman Publishers.

Brown, F., Driver, S. R., & Briggs, C. A. (2000). *Enhanced Brown-Driver-Briggs Hebrew and English Lexicon .* Oak Harbor: Logos Research Systems.

Butler, T. C. (2000). *Holman New Testament Commentary: Luke.* Nashville, TN: Broadman & Holman Publishers.

Calloway, B. A. (2015). *THE BOOK OF JAMES: CPH CHRISTIAN LIVING COMMENTARY.* Cambridge: Chriwstian Publishing House.

Clinton, T., & Ohlschlager, G. (2008). *Competent Christian Counseling; Volume One: Foundations and Practice of Compassionate Soul Care.* Colorado Springs, CO: WaterBrook Press.

Cole, R. D. (2000). *THE NEW AMERICAN COMMENTARY: Volume 3b Numbers.* Nashville: Broadman & Holman Publishers.

Cooper, L. E. (1994). *The New American Commentary, Ezekiel, vol. 17.* Nashville, TN: Broadman & Holman Publishers.

Cooper, R. (2000). *Holman New Testament Commentary: Mark.* Nashville: Broadman & Holman Publishers.

Corey, G. (2001). *Theory and Practice of Counseling and Psychotherapy, 6th ed.* Belmont, CA: Wadsworth.

Cornwall, J., & Smith, S. (1998). *The Exhaustive Dictionary of Bible Names.* Gainsville: Bridge-Logos.

Dockery, D. S. (1998). *HOLMAN CONCISE BIBLE COMMENTARY Simple, straightforward commentary on every book of the Bible.* Nashville: Broadman & Holman.

Easley, K. H. (1998). *Holman New Testament Commentary, vol. 12, Revelation.* (Nashville, TN: Broadman & Holman Publishers.

Easton, M. G. (1996, c1897). *Easton's Bible Dictionary.* Oak Harbor, WA: Logos Research Systems.

Edwards, T. (1908). *A Dictionary of Thoughts.* Detroit: F. B. Dickerson Company.

Elwell, W. A. (2001). *Evangelical Dictionary of Theology (Second Edition).* Grand Rapids: Baker Academic.

Elwell, W. A., & Comfort, P. W. (2001). *Tyndale Bible Dictionary.* Wheaton, Ill: Tyndale House Publishers.

Enns, P. P. (1997). *The Moody Handbook of Theology.* Chicago: Moody Press.

Erickson, M. J. (2001). *The Concise Dictionary of Christian Theology.* Wheaton: Crossway Books.

Erickson, M. J. (2013). *Christian Theology (Third Edition).* Grand Rapids, MI: Baker Academic.

Freedman, D. N., Myers, A. C., & Beck, A. B. (2000). *Eerdmans Dictionary of the Bible .* Grand Rapids, Mich.: W.B. Eerdmans .

Gangel, K. O. (1998). *Holman New Testament Commentary: Acts.* Nashville, TN: Broadman & Holman Publishers.

Gangel, K. O. (2000). *Holman New Testament Commentary, vol. 4, John .* Nashville, TN: Broadman & Holman Publishers.

Garland, D. E. (2003). *1 Corinthians, Baker Exegetical Commentary on the New Testament.* Grand Rapids, MI: : Baker Academic.

Garrett, D. A. (1993). *Proverbs, Ecclesiastes, Song of Songs, The New American Commentary, vol. 14.* Nashville: Broadman & Holman Publishers.

Garrett, D. A. (1993). *The New American Commentary: Vol. 14 (Proverbs, Ecclesiastes, Song of Songs).* Nashville: Broadman & Holman Publishers.

Geisler, N. L. (2003). *SYSTEMATIC THEOLOGY: God and Creation (Vol. 2).* Minneapolis: Baker Publishing Group.

Geisler, N. L. (2011). *Systematic Theology in One Volume.* Minneapolis, MN: Bethany House.

George, T. (2001). *The New American Commentary: Galatians .* Nashville, TN: Broadman & Holman Publishers.

Green, J. B., McKnight, S., & Marshall, H. (1992). *Dictionary of Jesus and the Gospels.* Downers Grove, IL: InterVarsity Press.

Grudem, W. (2011). *Making Sense of the Bible: One of Seven Parts from Grudem's Systematic Theology (Making Sense of Series).* Grand Rapids: Zondervan.

Hodge, C. (2003). *Systematic Theology 1.* Peabody: Hendrickson.

House, P. R. (2001). *The New American Commentary: Vol. 8., 2 Kings.* Nashville: Broadman & Holman Publishers.

Jean, A. (2003). *Words in the Mind: An Introduction to the Mental Lexicon - Third Edition.* Malden: Blackwell Publishing.

Kollar, C. A. (1997). *Solution-Focused Pastoral Counseling: An Effective Short-Term Approach for Getting People Back on Track.* Grand Rapids: Zondervan.

Larson, K. (2000). *Holman New Testament Commentary, vol. 9, I & II Thessalonians, I & II Timothy, Titus, Philemon.* Nashville, TN: Broadman & Holman Publishers.

Lea, T. D. (1999). *Holman New Testament Commentary: Vol. 10, Hebrews, James.* Nashville, TN: Broadman & Holman Publishers.

Lea, T. D., & Griffin, H. P. (1992). *The New American Commentary, vol. 34, 1, 2 Timothy, Titus.* Nashville: Broadman & Holman Publishers.

Lenski, R. C. (1945, 2008). *Interpretation of the I & II Epistles of Peter the Three Epistles of John, and the Epistle of Jude.* Minneapolis: Augsburg Fortress.

MacArthur, J. (2005). *Counseling: How to Counsel Biblically.* Nashville, TN: Thomas Nelson, Inc.

Marshall, T. F., & Andrews, E. D. (2022). *PAUL'S LETTER TO THE PHILIPPIANS: An Apologetic and Background Exposition of the Holy Scriptures.* Cambridge, Ohio: Christian publishing House.

Martin, D. M. (2001, c1995). *The New American Commentary 33 1, 2 Thessalonians .* Nashville, TN: Broadman & Holman.

Martin, G. S. (2002). *Holman Old Testament Commentary: Numbers.* Nashville: Broadman & Holman Publishers.

Mathews, K. A. (2001). *The New American Commentary vol. 1A, Genesis 1-11:26 .* Nashville: Broadman & Holman Publishers.

Matthews, K. A. (2001). *The New American Commentary Vol. 1B, Genesis 11:27-50:26.* Nashville: Broadman and Holman Publishers.

McMinn, M. R. (2010). *Psychology, Theology, and Spirituality in Christian Counseling (AACC Library).* Carol Stream, IL: Tyndale House Publishers.

Melick, R. R. (2001). *The New American Commentary: vol. 32, Philippians, Colissians, Philemon.* Nashville, TN : Broadman & Holman Publishers.

Microsoft. (1998-2010). *Encarta ® World English Dictionary.* Redmond: Microsoft Corporation. Retrieved April 10, 2010, from http://encarta.msn.com/encnet/features/dictionary/dictionaryhome.aspx

Mirriam-Webster, I. (2003). *Mirriam-Webster's Collegiate Dictionary. Eleventh Edition.* Springfield: Mirriam-Webster, Inc.

Mounce, R. H. (2001). *The New American Commentary: Vol. 27 Romans.* Nashville, TN: Broadman & Holman Publishers.

Mounce, R. H. (2001, c1995). *Romans: The New American Commentary 27.* Nashville: Broadman & Holman.

Mounce, W. D. (2006). *Mounce's Complete Expository Dictionary of Old & New Testament Words.* Grand Rapids, MI: Zondervan.

Myers, A. C. (1987). *The Eerdmans Bible Dictionary .* Grand Rapids, Mich: Eerdmans.

Polhill, J. B. (2001). *The New American Commentary 26: Acts.* Nashville: Broadman & Holman Publishers.

Pratt Jr, R. L. (2000). *Holman New Testament Commentary: I & II Corinthians, vol. 7.* Nashville: Broadman & Holman Publishers.

Richardson, K. (1997). *The New American Commentary Vol. 36 James.* Nashville: Broadman & Holman Publishers.

Rooker, M. F. (2000). *The New American Commentary, vol. 3A, Leviticus.* Nashville: Broadman & Holman Publishers.

Schreiner, T. R. (2003). *The New American Commentary: 1, 2 Peter, Jude.* Nashville: Broadman & Holman.

Smith, G. (2007). *The New American Commentary: Isaiah 1-39, Vol. 15a.* Nashville, TN: B & H Publishing Group.

Smith, G. (2009). *The New American Commentary: Isaiah 40-66, Vol. 15b.* Nashville, TN: B&H Publishing.

Stein, R. H. (2001, c1992). *The New American Commentary: Luke.* Nashville, TN: Broadman & Holman .

Stuart, D. K. (2006). *The New American Commentary: An Exegetical Theological Exposition of Holy Scripture EXODUS.* Nashville: Broadman & Holman.

Theissen, G. (1987). *Psychological aspects of Pauline Theology.* Philadelphia, PA: Fortress Press.

Vine, W. E. (1996). *Vine's Expository Dictionary of Old and New Testament Words.* Nashville: Thomas Nelson.

Voorhis, P. V., & Salisbury, E. J. (2013). *Correctional Counseling and Rehabilitation 8th Edition.* London: Routledge.

Walls, D., & Anders, M. (1996). *Holman New Testament Commentary: I & II Peter, I, II & III John, Jude.* Nashville: Broadman & Holman Publishers.

Watson, R. (1832). *A Biblical and Theological Dictionary: Explanatory of the History, Manners and Customs of the Jews.* New York: Waugh and T. Mason.

Weber, S. K. (2000). *Holman New Testament Commentary, vol. 1, Matthew.* Nashville, TN: Broadman & Holman Publishers.

Wood, D. R. (1996). *New Bible Dictionary (Third Edition).* Downers Grove: InterVarsity Press.

Zodhiates, S. (2000, c1992, c1993). *The Complete Word Study Dictionary: New Testament.* Chattanooga: AMG Publishers.

www.ingramcontent.com/pod-product-compliance
Lightning Source LLC
LaVergne TN
LVHW051739080426
835511LV00018B/3145